Wakefield Libraries
& Information Services

This book should be returned by the last date stamped above. You may renew the loan personally, by post or telephone for a further period if the book is not required by another reader.

LANCASHIRE'S SEASIDE PIERS

Also Featuring the Piers of the River Mersey, Cumbria and the Isle of Man

Martin Easdown

Wharncliffe Books

First published in Great Britain in 2009 by
Wharncliffe Books
An imprint of
Pen & Sword Books Ltd
47 Church Street
Barnsley
South Yorkshire
S70 2AS

ISBN 978 1 84563 093 5

A CIP catalogue record for this book is
available from the British Library

Typeset by Mac Style, Beverley, East Yorkshire
Printed and bound in the UK by CPI

Pen & Sword Books Ltd incorporates the Imprints of Pen & Sword
Aviation, Pen & Sword Maritime, Pen & Sword Military,
Wharncliffe Local History, Pen & Sword Select,
Pen & Sword Military Classics, Leo Cooper, Remember When,
Seaforth Publishing and Frontline Publishing

For a complete list of Pen & Sword titles please contact
PEN & SWORD BOOKS LIMITED
47 Church Street, Barnsley, South Yorkshire, S70 2AS, England
E-mail: enquiries@pen-and-sword.co.uk

Website: www.pen-and-sword.co.uk

CONTENTS

PREFACE

Following on from *Yorkshire's Seaside Piers*, published by Wharncliffe Books in 2008, we cross the Pennines to present the piers of Lancashire and the north-west. Whereas the Yorkshire book concentrated on just six pleasure piers, so allowing for an in-depth study of each pier, this book covers a wider spectrum of twenty-eight piers and landing stages.

The Lancashire resorts were at the forefront of building pleasure piers and every major resort in the county built itself a pier; with early examples being erected at Southport and Blackpool. The resorts flourished during the Victorian times, particularly Blackpool, as the Lancashire coast became the principal holiday destination for the workers of the nearby industrial towns during their Wakes Weeks. Blackpool's popularity ensured that it could build three piers (two further piers were proposed but not built). Morecambe, which was particularly popular with people from the West Riding of Yorkshire, tried to rival Blackpool in the number of attractions and piers offered and built two piers. Southport considered itself a bit more select and built the second longest pier in the country, complete with a pier train. The genteel resorts of Lytham and St Annes each erected a pier, while the pier at Fleetwood was built right at the end of the pier-building age. The famous inland 'non-pier' at Wigan was the butt of many a music hall joke and was made further famous by the George Orwell book *The Road to Wigan Pier*.

On the opposite side of the Mersey in Cheshire, New Brighton was developed as the seaside resort for Liverpool, and as well as a pier, boasted a tower taller than Blackpool's. A number of other Mersey ferry stopping points on the Cheshire side of the river built substantial pier structures related to their seaside cousins; now mostly gone.

The Isle of Man was another popular holiday destination, particularly with people from Lancashire for whom it was within easy reach. Two pleasure piers were built on the island: the short-lived Iron Pier at Douglas and Ramsey's Queens Pier whose main function was as a landing stage. The present-day Cumbrian coast has never been popular enough to support a fully-fledged pleasure pier, although two small landing piers were erected at Grange-over-Sands; a small stone pier at Arnside whilst Silloth boasted a substantial wooden harbour pier used for promenading.

Sadly, many of the piers featured in this book are no more. Douglas Iron Pier was removed as long ago as 1894 to be re-erected at Rhos-on-

Sea in north Wales, whilst the island's other pier at Ramsey has been closed for over a decade as debates continue as what to do with it. Morecambe's two piers have also been consigned to history, although its fine stone jetty remains as some kind of consolation. Grange's two little wooden piers are long-lost, yet fortunately the attractive little stone pier at nearby Arnside is alive and well. Lytham Pier was demolished in 1960 and the recent demise by fire of Fleetwood highlighted the continuing vulnerability of piers. Only Rock Ferry remains of the substantial iron piers that once graced the Cheshire side of the River Mersey.

Nevertheless five fine piers continue to grace the Lancashire coast. Of Blackpool's three piers, the North Pier is the outstanding structure with its traditional wide, open promenade deck, attractive kiosks and pier theatre. Central and South Piers are now largely given over to amusements but remain successful structures in their own right. St Annes Pier is a truncated shadow of its former self, yet the pier's under deck ironwork is outstanding and its entrance building beguiling. Southport Pier, the second longest pleasure pier in the country, has recently been restored complete with a new pier tram and is a fine testament to the confidence shown in the future of the seaside pleasure pier.

Martin Easdown
2009

CHAPTER ONE

PLEASURE UPON THE IRISH SEA

The Evolution of the Lancashire Seaside Towns and their Piers

The foundation of the great British seaside has been laid claim to by amongst others Scarborough (with its existing seaside spa), Weymouth (patronage of George III), Margate (boat connection with London) and Brighton, favoured by the Prince Regent and London Society. However it could be argued that it was on the Lancashire coast and Blackpool in particular, that the zenith of resort development had been reached by the dawn of the twentieth century. Blackpool and New Brighton (in Cheshire but with the majority of its custom emanating from the Lancashire side of the Mersey) boasted the only two seaside Eiffel Towers in Britain. All the major resorts had at least one pier, although Morecambe had two and Blackpool three. Theatres, winter gardens, amusements and pleasure palaces abounded around the north-west coast in New Brighton, Southport, Lytham, St Annes-on-Sea, Blackpool, Morecambe and Douglas, Isle of Man.

Lancashire was at the forefront of the Industrial Revolution of the nineteenth century and its seaside resorts boasted a ready market from the large industrial towns nearby, such as Liverpool, Manchester, Preston, Blackburn and Bolton. The area had the greatest concentration of regularly paid workers during a period of rising living standards. The Wakes Week tradition flourished in Lancashire where factories, shops and even whole towns closed up for their annual holiday to the seaside. Although the Bank Holiday Act of 1871 stipulated that Whit Monday, Easter Monday, Boxing Day and the first Monday in August should join Good Friday and Christmas Day as public holidays, paid holidays were an exception. To pay for the holiday by the seaside, workers joined Wakes saving clubs (otherwise known as 'going away clubs') established at their place of work into which they paid a small amount each week. The Wakes Week tradition was summed up by local historian Stella Davies in 1963:

> Wakes Weeks are staggered, each town in the industrial area taking different weeks throughout the summer for their annual holiday. The overwhelming majority of people went to Blackpool, although some, eccentrically, went to Morecambe or even Rhyl. Blackpool therefore, was full at any one time,

with neighbours from the same town, and no-one need feel isolated or lonely. Groups of relatives and friends would share lodgings or take them in the same street and young and old, children, courting couples and married folk alike, would spend a year's savings in one glorious spree.

The journey to the resorts from the industrial towns was made by rail. Lancashire had one of the densest railway systems in the country, which had a considerable impact on the development of its resorts. The earliest railway to the Lancashire coast was the Preston and Wyre Railway, opened in 1840 to serve Sir Peter Hesketh-Fleetwood's new port and resort of Fleetwood. The North Euston Hotel was built for passengers awaiting their boat connection to Scotland and Decimus Burton designed an elegant new town, of which only a few terraces were built. The scheme bankrupted Hesketh-Fleetwood and it was to be Blackpool and Lytham that was to gain from the Preston and Wyre Railway when branches were opened to these expanding resorts in 1846. Two years later, Morecambe (then known as Poulton-le-Sands) gained its railway and Southport was connected to Liverpool. In 1855 a line was opened from Southport to Wigan, which brought it within easy reach of the industrial heartland.

Southport was one of the earliest of the Lancashire resorts dating back to 1792 with the opening of a small hotel on the shore. By 1820 it was an established resort for sea bathing and its famous shopping street, Lord Street, was developed from the 1840s. A small jetty was erected in 1850 but was replaced by Lancashire's first fully-fledged seaside pier ten years later.

By the 1860s, piers were being erected for use as promenades over the sea as well as landing stages. Durable cast iron and decorative wrought iron had largely superseded wood as the preferred method of building material for piers and screw piling ensured a solid foundation for the pier supports. The Piers and Harbours Act of 1861 eased the process of promoting pier schemes, and the introduction of limited liability did the same for shareholders wishing to invest in pier companies.

Southport was the second seaside pier to be built of iron and one of the earliest pleasure piers. The pier also came to be the second longest, in order to reach the deep water channel of the sea, which was already beginning to desert the resort. A tramway was opened in 1864 to convey customers along the pier and in 1867–8 the structure was further extended to 4,380ft. The pier was promoted as a select promenade, yet Southport in general led rather a schizophrenic life as a seaside resort. On the one hand was the genteel aspect of Lord Street, the large hotels and the well-maintained gardens, yet the excellent rail links also brought the trippers to the fairground on the beach.

Blackpool's origins as a seaside resort began humbly in the 1780s when two inns catered for the few visitors arriving to enjoy the golden sands. The opening of the railway to the town in 1846 proved to be the impetus for development as excursionists began to arrive in increasing numbers, and by the early 1850s Blackpool was playing host to some 12,000 working–class visitors during an August weekend. As at Southport, a pier was an early attraction, opening in 1863. A second pier followed in 1868, opened by a breakaway faction from the first pier. The two piers soon began to cater for different markets: the first pier (the North Pier) for select market, the South Jetty (later the Central Pier) for the trippers.

The real flourishing of Blackpool commenced from the 1870s under the enterprising nature of the corporation and the local businessmen who controlled the leisure industry. The corporation actively advertised the charms of the town, particularly at railway stations and in 1883 Blackpool had 1,300,000 arrivals by train. Innovative use of the new-fangled electric power saw illuminations strung along the promenade in 1879 and the opening of Britain's first electric street tramway in 1885. Lack of a large local land owner to control development meant that Blackpool developed piecemeal with terraced rows of red-brick houses (mirroring the houses of the town's visitors), public houses and amusements on the seafront.

A serious rival to the Blackpool piers appeared in 1877 with the opening of the Winter Gardens with its all-day, all-weather attractions. This led to the North Pier being enlarged and a splendid Indian Pavilion being added on the pier head. A third pier, the Victoria (later South) Pier was opened in 1893, which initially tried to outdo the North Pier for selectiveness. The apogee of leisure provision in Blackpool was reached in 1894 with the opening of the Tower and by the Edwardian period the town had fully outstripped all of its rivals with the number of attractions offered. By the outbreak of the First World War in 1914 nearly four million visitors per year were coming to Blackpool. The resort was a magnet for organised excursions, which often came on Sundays. The Bass Brewery at Burton-upon-Trent ran their first trip to Blackpool in 1885 and was so popular the number of trains had to be increased from six to eight and a ninth could have been filled if the railway company could have provided it. In 1900 11,241 people went on the Bass trip to Blackpool and in 1907 seventeen trains had to be provided (which were staggered throughout the day necessitating a tremendous feat of organisation).

Morecambe made a determined effort to rival Blackpool around the turn of the twentieth century with the addition of the Kings Theatre to the

Winter Gardens, a new West End Pier, a total rebuild of the existing Central Pier, a failed tower and the Alhambra Theatre. Reliance on their Yorkshire catchment area, however, and the longer travelling distance from the Lancashire cotton towns meant Morecambe could still only attract a tenth of Blackpool's numbers. The two piers sported impressive pavilions, with that on the Central Pier earning the sobriquet, the 'Taj Mahal of the North'. During the 1880s and 1890s many piers added pavilions, theatres and other amusements to compete with shore-based attractions.

The working-class of Liverpool had their own seaside playground at New Brighton, just across the other side of the Mersey. Originally conceived in the 1830s as a select watering place and residential suburb for the wealthy of Merseyside, by the 1890s New Brighton was actively catering for the hordes of trippers arriving on the ferries and by train. The promenade pier of 1866 erected a pavilion in 1892 to present variety entertainment and in addition offered divers and slot machines. In 1900, the New Brighton Tower complex was opened close to the pier, which boasted an array of attractions on par with its Blackpool namesake and a tower that was over 100ft higher. Eastham, with its pleasure gardens, and Rock Ferry's Olympian Gardens provided further attractions on the Cheshire side of the Mersey.

The more adventurous holidaymaker looked beyond the Lancashire coast to the Isle of Man, which by 1870 was receiving 60,000 visitors annually. The island's capital, Douglas, was also the main arrival point and seaside resort and a promenade pier was erected in 1869. However the provision of large entertainment complexes and theatres during the 1880s and 1890s effectively crowded the pier out and it was sold and dismantled in 1894. Ramsey was the only other place on the island to build a pier, principally to serve the steamer trade.

Lytham and St Annes-on-Sea were quieter alternatives to their boisterous Blackpool neighbour. The old settlement of Lytham blossomed during the first part of the nineteenth century into a quiet seaside resort known for its green on the seafront and many trees, earning it the designation 'Leafy Lytham'. A pier, albeit rather a plain one, was erected in 1865 and mirrored its resort in its gentility. St Annes-on-Sea was a purpose-built resort instigated by the St Annes Land and Building Company to *secure a more select, better class of visitor*. Villas and hotels were erected in uniform east Lancashire stone. A pier was completed in 1885, but was to remain a rather plain structure until transformed between 1899 and 1910 with the addition of the beautiful Moorish Pavilion, a gabled entrance building and a floral hall.

Grange-over-Sands was the quietest and most select of the Lancashire resorts. Situated on the edge of the Lake District in 'Lancashire O'er the Water', Grange was a health resort for the well-off, and genteel amusements such as bandstands, were provided. Two small piers catered for boat trips around Morecambe Bay but a silting-up of the channels put paid to the sailings and the piers were demolished.

The serenity of Grange seemed a million miles away from the brashness of Blackpool, yet this eclectic mixture of resorts along the Lancashire coast proved to be an enticing arcadia for all classes of Lancashire life. A Wonderland awaited them.

CHAPTER TWO

THE FERRY PIERS OF THE RIVER MERSEY

New Brighton – Egremont – Seacombe – Woodside – Monks Ferry – Birkenhead – Tranmere — Rock Ferry – New Ferry – Eastham – Liverpool Pier Head (St George's Landing Stage) – Liverpool South End

There has been a ferry service between the important commercial centre of Liverpool and the Wirral Peninsula on the opposite side of the River Mersey since at least the eleventh century when the Domesday Book of 1086 recorded a crossing between Liverpool and Seacombe (at the narrowest point of the river). After the establishment of Birkenhead Priory in 1150, the monks used to row people across the river for a small fee, which was legalised by a royal charter granted by Edward III on 13 April 1330.[1] The same monarch also granted the Earl of Chester the right to operate a ferry from Seacombe and Birkenhead, thus establishing the Wallasey Ferry. By the sixteenth century, ferries were running from Seacombe, Birkenhead (Woodside), Tranmere and Eastham to Liverpool.

The growth of Liverpool as a commercial centre during the latter half of the eighteenth century and early nineteenth century saw the expansion of both passenger and goods traffic across the river, with passenger sailings often meeting the stage coach service from Chester. Services had commenced from Rock Ferry by 1709 and New Ferry in 1774 and these often connected with the Chester coaches.

The sailing vessels which had originally provided the ferry services began to be replaced by steamers from 1815 when the wooden paddle steamer *Elizabeth* operated between Liverpool and Runcorn. During the 1840s Birkenhead was expanding fast with the opening of the railway from Chester and the building of the docks and the town had four competing ferry services to Liverpool from Woodside, Monk's Ferry, Birkenhead and Tranmere. Services had also commenced from the recently founded Wallasey watering place of New Brighton and from nearby Egremont. There were also sailings from Liverpool to Ellesmere Port and Runcorn and a service from the South-End stage at Liverpool to New Ferry. The services from Liverpool and Widnes to Runcorn finished soon after 1854 when the ferry was purchased by the St Helens Railway and Canal Company for the sum of £920 per annum. The success of the well-used ferries led to the busiest coming under municipal ownership, commencing with the Birkenhead Commissioners acquisition of Woodside in 1858. In 1861 the Wallasey Local Board took over the three ferries in its area, New Brighton, Egremont and Seacombe. The Birkenhead fleet, which sported red and black funnels were named in honour of local places, whilst the Wallasey ferries, with their black and white funnels, were called after both local places and flowers. In 1879, luggage boats were introduced to carry goods and vehicles across the river.

The supremacy of the ferries was first challenged in 1886 with the opening of the 1230 yard long Mersey Railway Tunnel. By 1894, the tunnel was carrying 25,000 passengers compared to the 44,000 using the ferries. However it was the opening of the Queensway road tunnel in 1934 that heralded a sharp decline in the use of the ferries. Seacombe Ferry lost two million passengers to the road tunnel and the luggage boats saw an 80% reduction in usage which saw their withdrawal from service in the 1940s. Birkenhead Corporation closed its southern terminals at New Ferry (1927), Eastham (1929) and Rock Ferry (1939) and Wallesey attempted to close Egremont. Local pressure kept the ferry open but in 1941 it was closed after the pier was damaged by a vessel.

Heavy post-war patronage of the ferries saw 30 million passengers use it in 1950, but during the subsequent decade numbers began to decline. In 1956 the night ferries were withdrawn in favour of buses through the tunnel.

The passing of the Transport Act in 1968 saw the Merseyside Passenger Transport Executive (MPTE) take control of the Mersey ferries on 1 December 1969. However, by 1970 only seven million people were using the ferries each year and this was to decline even further upon the opening of the Kingsway road tunnel on 28 June 1971. New Brighton Ferry was closed in 1971 and the future of remaining Seacombe and Woodside ferries was cast into doubt. The service frequency was reduced, and in 1977 a bill was placed before parliament to discontinue ferry services altogether. However, public sentiment and affection for the ferries staved off complete closure. Nevertheless commuter traffic could no longer sustain the service alone, which by 1989 was running at an annual deficit of £2.5 million. This led to the current operators, Merseytravel, re-branding the ferries from 1990 as a heritage and visitor attraction.

Three vessels: *Royal Iris of the Mersey* (formerly *Mountwood*), *Snowdrop* (ex-*Woodchurch*) and *Royal Daffodil* (formerly *Overchurch*) are used to operate an hourly summer triangular service between Liverpool, Seacombe and Woodside, which are marketed as Mersey Ferries River Explorer Cruises. Recently the Mersey Ferries fleet underwent a £10.5 million refurbishment programme. Families are encouraged to use the ferries by the provision of the £9 million Spaceport attraction at Seacombe, and the placing of German U-boat U-534 is planned for Woodside. The ferries also operate charter cruises and a Manchester Ship Canal cruise. During Liverpool's European Capital of Culture celebrations in 2008 the three ferries saw heavy patronage, particularly during the Tall Ships weekend of 18–21 July.

NEW BRIGHTON

Situated on the tip of the Wirral, New Brighton was the playground and seaside resort for the working class of Liverpool. The resort was famous for boasting the tallest building in England for a time with the building of a tower in 1898 that was 621ft high, over 100ft higher than its rival at Blackpool.

James Atherton (1770–1838), a merchant, property dealer and developer, 'born to be busy' and an 'ardent, bold and daring character' was chiefly responsible for the creation of New Brighton. Atherton lived in the Liverpool suburb of Everton and could view the tip of the Wirral Peninsula with the fine golden sands of the Black Rock. He considered it ripe for development as a select watering place, having carried out the expansion of fine terraced houses and villas in Everton. In 1830, in conjunction with his son-in-law William Rowson (1791–1863) he began negotiations with John Penkett, Lord of the Manor of Liscard, to buy a large section of headland at the north-eastern tip of the Wirral Peninsula. On 24 January 1832, a deposit of £200 (£100 each from Atherton and Rowson) was advanced towards the purchase of 170 acres of the 'New Brighton Estate', which was to cost a total of £27,289.

The two men built grand houses for themselves and laid out a road system for the transportation of building materials. Montpelier Crescent and Albion Street were amongst the earliest streets developed, situated on gently undulating land allowing each villa an uninterrupted sea view of Liverpool Bay, framed by the Welsh hills to the west and the Lancashire coast to the east. It was hoped the new town would have a three-fold attraction: as a residential dormitory for the professional classes of Liverpool, a summer retreat for the wealthy and as a select watering place. Healthy sea air, golden sands and safe bathing were all promoted as incentives for choosing to live or stay in New Brighton.

The two most prominent landmarks the new resort possessed at that time were the Perch Rock Battery, a red sandstone fort guarding the entrance into Liverpool Bay, opened on 30 April 1829 and the Perch Rock Lighthouse opened on 1 March 1830. Both remain as very distinctive features of New Brighton today.

In October 1832, Atherton and Rowson produced a prospectus to invite investors to buy shares at £100 each in order that a hotel and ferry link to Liverpool could be established. Land was also offered for development and Rowson set up a flourishing brickmaking business to supply the bricks for the villas in the course of erection. Both the hotel and a rather crude wooden landing stage for the ferry service were opened in March 1834. Rowson designed an unusual landing stage comprising of a 135ft pier facing north-east before it deviated south for a further 40ft. At low tide however, passengers had to wade through the water to the stage or were carried in a flat bottomed boat. An hourly service was advertised to Liverpool using the vessel *Sir John Moore*, which took twenty-five minutes (in good weather) to do the journey.

Following James Atherton's death in 1838, his sons maintained the ferry service from New Brighton until 1845. The rights then passed to Messrs Lodge Pritchard & Company, which included two of the dynamic Coulborn brothers, William and Edward, as directors. They added a small movable 200ft run out stage to the pier worked by a windlass

The first New Brighton ferry pier, photographed in about 1860. Opened in 1834, the pier was too short to be used at low tide and passengers often had to wade through the water to reach the shore. At the entrance to the pier can be seen a refreshment room. Marlinova Collection

propelled by a horse. When the ebb tide set in, each ferry boat as she departed pulled the stage out into the river a sufficient distance to allow for her to dock by it by the time she returned on her next trip. There was also a long flight of steps between the landing stage and the shore, up and down which the toll collector carried a small pay box on his back to use whether the passengers were landing on the pier at high water or onto the shore at low water. At the entrance to the pier was a refreshment room and on the pier head a small hut. The new additions to the pier cost around £3,000, and in addition the steamers *Queen of Beauty* and *James Atherton* were acquired for the New Brighton route. The *Queen of Beauty* was a former yacht that operated at New Brighton from 1845 to 1856 providing a luxury service for the town's more wealthy residents and visitors.

A plan in 1848 to greatly extend the pier failed to come to fruition and the same year saw the shore end damaged in a gale. The Coulborns took over the running of Egremont Ferry in May 1848 and suspended the New Brighton service in the winter of 1849–50 to save money. Upon the reopening of New Brighton, its services were combined with those at Egremont.

New Brighton's ferry and promenade piers pictured on a carte-de-visite c.1870. At this time the only entrance to the promenade pier was via the ferry pier. The new ferry pier was opened in 1866, followed by the promenade pier a year later. Marlinova Collection

New Brighton Ferry proved to be the most profitable of the three Wallasey ferries, particularly during the summer months. During 1859 for example, receipts at New Brighton were £9,042, compared with £6,134 at Seacombe and £5,390 at Egremont.

The Coulborns ran all three Wallasey ferries until 1 August 1861 when, under the provisions of the Wallasey Improvement Acts of 1858 and 1861, the Wallasey Local Board purchased the New Brighton and Egremont ferries for £60,000 and acquired the rights of passage for Seacombe for £30,000. A half-hourly service was provided on all three passages, although New Brighton's was reduced to an hour during the winter and it was closed on Sundays.

The problem of landing at the New Brighton stage at low tide continued to be a problem and the old run-out stage was often unreliable. There was no other option for the council than to totally renew the stage, and powers for its construction were included in the Wallasey Improvement Act 1864. The council chose the design of James Brunlees for an iron pier (which was also used for New Ferry Pier) for the ferry, which incorporated a floating landing stage drawn up by William Carson, Manager of Wallasey Ferries since 1863. The new pier was to be sited slightly to the north-east of its predecessor, which enabled the old structure to still be used whilst its replacement was under construction. Messrs Peto, Brassey and Potts of Birkenhead were initially awarded the contract to build the pier, but they realised that the estimated completion date of 1 July 1865 would prove to be unattainable so on 5 January 1865 the contract was transferred to Rothwell & Company of Bolton. Curiously the council decided not to have Brunlees as engineer-in-charge of the project and chose their own engineer instead. This decision was to ensure that the building of the pier was to be fraught with problems. One such problem was when the connecting bridge to the floating pontoon collapsed whilst being placed in position, causing the pontoon to break up and deposit 200 people into the water, fortunately without loss of life. Rothwell & Company were replaced for the 'inadequacy of their work' by Messrs Bowdler & Chaffer, the Seacombe shipbuilders and on 20 May 1866 the new pier was finally opened. The final cost of the pier was £23,906, far more than the original estimate of £9,250.

The landing stage of the new pier was of an innovative floating design of some 200ft in length and 30ft in breadth and was connected to the pier by a 160ft iron bridge. Twelve large iron pontoons enabled the landing stage to rise and fall with the tide. The main body of the pier measured 600ft and consisted of wrought-iron girders resting on cast iron columns, strengthened horizontally by angle irons and vertically by 3in iron bracing bars.

Unfortunately, the bridge and floating landing stage were wrecked by the screw steamer *Galileo* during a gale on 3 October 1867. The landward end of the bridge was wrenched from its moorings and the landing stage floated out into the river where it was rescued by the ferry boats *Wallasey* and *Waterlily*.[2] Repairs were carried out at a cost of £3,850 and the landing stage was reopened on 28 May 1868, although work to anchor it more securely to the sea bed continued into 1869. Nevertheless the lack of water at low tide remained a problem and occasionally boats had to be hired for use as an extension to the stage.

Meanwhile, on 25 July 1864, the New Brighton Promenade Pier Company was incorporated with a capital of £30,000 (3,000 shares of £10) to erect a promenade pier alongside the ferry pier, and the design of Eugenius Birch for a pier was chosen. Birch was the top name in pier design during the 1860s, having already designed by 1866 piers at Margate, Blackpool, Deal, Brighton, Lytham, Aberystwyth, Eastbourne and Scarborough. His New Brighton Pier was unusual in that it could only be reached via the ferry pier not directly from the shore. The pier platform measured 550ft x 130ft, and an upper promenade deck was also provided measuring 180ft x 20ft. The contractor chosen to build the pier was Joseph Dowson, who had assisted Birch on the pier at Aberystwyth. Dowson fixed the first column of the pier on 19 December 1866.

The construction of the pier progressed relatively smoothly, enabling it to be ready to open to the public on 7 September 1867. A report on the opening appeared in the *Illustrated London News*:

Emulating the example of other watering places, the rising town of New Brighton has added to its former attractions that of a promenade pier, which is to be opened to the public this day. New Brighton is situated on the Cheshire side of the Mersey, near its outlet to the sea; and, whilst it is a kind of marine suburb to the town of Liverpool, also enjoys, with Blackpool and Southport, a fair share of the patronage of pleasure-seeking and health-seeking visitors from Manchester and other manufacturing towns. The pier was commenced for the New Brighton Pier Company in the autumn of last year, and the works have been proceeded with in so expeditious a manner as to enable the company to open it to the public much earlier than was anticipated. It is similar in its construction to the piers at Blackpool, Brighton, and elsewhere, which have been erected within the last few years, from the designs and under the superintendence of the same engineer.

The pier is supported upon 120 columns, firmly fixed in the rocky foundations. Four lines of longitudinal main girders run throughout the entire length of the pier, braced diagonally and transversely with wrought-iron beams fixed to the main girders, and upon these are laid planks, wedged and bolted and covered with close planking, to afford an even and comfortable promenade. Along the entire length of the pier sitting accommodation is provided. The area of the pier is between 50,000 and 60,000 superficial feet. There is a handsome saloon, with ornamental houses available for shelter and as refreshment rooms and bazaars. From the centre tower over the saloon and the galleries over the houses magnificent views are obtained of the shipping in the River Mersey and the vessels passing to and from Liverpool. A handsome orchestra is provided for the band, and there are weather-screens similar to those erected at Brighton New Pier for the first time, which have been highly appreciated by the public.

The entrance to the pier is by a flight of steps, 30ft in width, from the gangway of the landing-pontoon recently erected by the Wallasey Commissioners.

Admission to the pier was 2d, although the upper deck was an additional 1d. From the upper deck, a Byzantine central tower could be reached where telescopes were placed. The work was not fully completed until the following year, when on 9 April 1868 the pier was officially handed over to the pier company having cost £27,000 to build.

In the years 1861 to 1881 the population of New Brighton grew from 1,092 to 5,665 as smaller terraced houses for those with a more moderate pocket filled in the gaps between Atherton's villas. The town was also attracting increasing numbers of visitors. Victoria Road became New Brighton's main shopping street and the Palace and Winter Gardens its first major entertainment venue. Opened in 1882, the Palace featured salt water baths, a skating rink, an aquarium, grotto, aviary and two concert halls, all available for the inclusive price of 6d.[3] Atherton's aspirations of a select watering place were replaced by the resort becoming the playground of working-class Liverpool and Birkenhead, assisted by the opening of the Mersey Railway to New Brighton in 1888. By 1890 the beach was home to all manner of trades such as swings, side shows, beach hawkers, bathing machines, refreshment stalls and donkeys. In that year the Wallasey Local Board found it necessary to designate the foreshore as a public highway and regulate 'the erection or placing or continuance on the foreshore or the approaches thereto or any parts thereof of any booths, tents, sheds, stands, stalls, shows, exhibitions, performances, swings, roundabouts, fishing stakes, wreckage or other erections or things, vans, photographic carts or other vehicles whether drawn or propelled by animals or persons, and the playing of any games on the foreshore.' In addition they felt compounded to regulate 'the selling and hawking of any article, commodity or thing on the foreshore, and any part thereof for riding and driving'. Nevertheless some sixty female hawkers continued to operate on the beach by the pier. They crossed the Mersey from Liverpool and from their wicker baskets sold New Brighton rock, postcards, strings of shells and beads, paper windmills, food and drink. Some even sold cages of love birds. These tough breed of women were known as 'Mary Ellens' and clubbed together to pay each others' fines for hawking on the beach.

The rise in popularity of New Brighton led to the ferry pier being badly congested during the summer months. In October 1879 plans for a new landing stage 240ft x 55ft and a second passenger bridge were drawn by J & EA Dowson at a projected cost of £6,500, but a backlash from ratepayers meant the plan was put on hold. A modified scheme by Dowson was prepared two years later for a 220ft long stage and the contract to build it was awarded in 1884 to Head, Wrightson & Company who had submitted a tender of £7,327. The work was completed the following year, but further repairs had to be carried out within a few years and in 1896 the consulting engineer JJ Webster declared that the ferry pier was in need of urgent repairs. A new north passenger bridge (replacing the original of 1866) was put in place in 1900, although a proposal in 1899 to widen the whole of the ferry pier was modified to just widening a small section around the kiosks. Various schemes to lengthen the pier never came to fruition and Wallasey Council often had

A postcard showing the promenade and ferry piers at New Brighton during the Edwardian period. The card was posted to Glasgow in August 1914 just as the Great War was beginning. The promenade pier gained its own entrance from the shore in 1900 and a banner on the toll house is advertising the Great Cycle Dive.
Marlinova Collection

to dredge the sand around the pier head to enable the ferries to continue to call. The paddle steamer *Thistle* and former Birkenhead luggage vessel *Woodside* (renamed *Shamrock*) were added to the Wallasey fleet in 1891 although the latter proved unsatisfactory and was sold in March 1902. Three further vessels were added in 1895: the coal barge *Emily* and the identical paddle steamers *Pansy* and *John Herron* (named in honour of the ferry committee chairman). Pleasure steamers of the Southport, Preston and Blackpool Steam Packet Company and the Birkdale, Southport and Preston Steamship Company occasionally called at the ferry pier on route from Liverpool to North Wales.

A rather plain pavilion was added to the promenade pier in 1892, which was described as a covered saloon 130ft in length and varying in width from 28–34ft, in use for concerts, balls, bazaars and flower shows. The engagement of Adeler & Sutton's Pierrots in the Pier Pavilion from 1898 brought good crowds onto the pier. A further attraction was Professor JO Matchett of Liverpool performing his Great Cycle Dive off the pier. In 1899–1900 the promenade pier was finally extended to a length of 660ft to reach the new promenade. It now had its own separate entrance, although the entry from the ferry pier was retained. The work was carried out in conjunction with the newly extended promenade laid between Holland Road and Victoria Road. Refurbishment work on the pavilion was carried out in 1909–10 which included complete redecoration and the installation of new heating.

New Brighton was at the zenith of its growth and popularity at the dawn of the twentieth century with the opening of the tower complex with its huge ballroom, circus, amusement park and of course the tower itself, the tallest building in England at 621ft. There was also the notorious Ham and Egg Parade, a row of shops and cafes close to the pier, where the rough and tough element hung out. Such was its bad reputation the council pulled it down in 1907 to build the Victoria Gardens and Floral Pavilion and widen the promenade. The same year saw the opening of the Winter Garden Theatre in the Alexandra Hall[4] and in 1914 the Tivoli Theatre was added on the Tower Promenade.[5]

The ferry pier met with an accident on 16 March 1907 when the north bridge of the landing stage collapsed, causing the pontoon to float for some distance down the river. The southern bridge was also badly damaged and a replacement, built by Heenan and Froude of Manchester, was installed on 29 August 1907. Passengers using the ferry continued to grow with an increase of 17,209,537 in 1904 to 22,537,909 in 1913. The landing stage was renewed again in 1920–1 with the addition of a new gangway at a cost of £25,691. An all year service was inaugurated that year, which lasted until 1936 when it cut back to Easter and summer

The promenade pier at New Brighton following its reconstruction by Wallasey Council in 1928–30. New additions to the pier included the circular pavilion and a bandstand. Marlinova Collection

The floating landing stage of the New Brighton ferry pier c.1935 with the *J Farley* having discharged its passengers. The *J Farley* was in service on the Mersey from 1922 to 1952. Marlinova Collection

only. Ferries used on the thirty-minute crossing included the *Iris* (later *Royal Iris*)[6] from 1906–23 and summer trips to 1931; *Daffodil* (later *Royal Daffodil*) 1906–31 and summer trips to 1933; *John Joyce* (originally *Bluebell* and named in honour of the chairman of the Ferries Committee) 1910–36; *Snowdrop* 1910–36; *Francis Storey* 1922–51 and *J. Farley* 1922–52.

However by the 1920s the promenade pier was in need of attention and the pier company could ill-afford the repairs. The pavilion was closed in 1923 and the pier was later declared unsafe by the Board of Trade. The Wallasey Corporation Act of 1927 empowered the corporation to acquire the pier for £13,000 and they carried out a complete refurbishment under the management of EJA Shaw. Rusted girders and bracing were replaced with steel components and reinforcing collars were added to the damaged piles. On the pier deck, the old pavilion was demolished and a bandstand, lounge and clubhouse for the West Cheshire Sailing Club were added. The council spent a total of £45,000 on the pier, enabling it to reopen in 1930. A number of improvements were carried out to the ferry pier during the winter of 1935–6, including the widening of the deck, the placing of extra supporting columns and a new booking hall.

During the Second World War the pier was requisitioned as a searchlight battery site and torpedo tubes were installed on the landing stage to protect the entry into Liverpool. At the war's end the periscope of a German submarine was placed on the pier and for a small charge customers could view the Mersey shipping through the eyes of a U boat commander.

Both the promenade and ferry piers largely maintained their popularity during the 1950s and early 1960s. In 1959–60 a new steel north bridge costing £42,000 was added to the ferry pier by Messrs Wilton and Bell of London Wall. The south bridge was reconstructed and a new concrete bridgehead was built. However, on 11 January 1962 the north bridge was lifted from its shore end pintle during a gale and collided with the south bridge before falling into the sea. The north bridge was able to be repaired at a cost of £12,000, but a new south bridge had to be provided at a cost of £64,881. The condition of the promenade pier was also causing concern and in 1965 it was closed by the council. The decline in the fortunes of the pier mirrored those of the resort. The golden sands had been lost as Liverpool Docks expanded and the Seaforth complex altered currents creating a polluting, muddy foreshore.

A subsidiary of Trust House Forte took over the running of the promenade pier and reopened it in 1968. Facilities on the pier at this time were a pavilion, waltzer, octopus ride, amusement arcade, Trabant ride, dodgems, bingo arcade, ice cream stall and souvenir stalls and shops. An estimated £200,000 was spent on improvements but the pier

New Brighton promenade pier pictured in 1973, a year after the structure had been closed. Demolition of the adjoining ferry pier was started that year and was completed in 1974. The promenade pier was never to reopen and was demolished in 1978. Marlinova Collection

still ran at a loss and it was closed again in 1972. The ferry pier was by this time redundant with the last ferry having left on 26 September 1971: passenger numbers using the ferry had fallen from an annual figure of three million in 1953 to just 300,000. Demolition of the ferry pier was commenced in September 1973 and was completed in October 1974. In 1977, the Government granted approval for the demolition of the promenade pier, which was completed the following year.

In 2002, a three-phase regeneration plan was announced for the sea front which was to include a new 500ft pier on the site of the original at a cost of £3.4 million. The proposals were put forward by Neptune Developments Ltd, a Liverpool-based property company; however, by 2008 no pier had yet appeared.

Where the site the promenade and ferry piers met the shore is partially covered by a water treatment building, which is marked out by the words 'Pier'.

EGREMONT

The original ferry landing stage at Egremont was built in 1830 by Captain John Askew, Harbour Master of Liverpool, who had built a fine villa in the area and named it after his home town in Cumberland. Captain Askew was assisted by Sir John Tobin, the Lord Mayor of Liverpool and in 1830 he purchased from the Crown the lease rights for a ferry for £3,000. A ferry landing stage was built of wood but could only be used at high tide as it was just 200ft long: the gently sloping nature of the shore necessitated that a pier of some 750ft in length would be needed to enable vessels to call at all states of the tide. A second-hand paddle steamer *Loch Ech* was purchased in August 1830 and a service to Liverpool was commenced. The *John Rigby* was added in 1831 and the *Hero* in 1832.

However, the service was frequently suspended when the vessels were required for towing duties and in October 1835 the ferry passed to the Egremont Steam Ferry Company which had been formed with a capital of £10,000. Askew however retained ownership of the land and financed a 50ft extension to the landing stage. The company acquired three new vessels to operate the ferry: *Ennishowen* (1836), *Egremont* (1837) and *Thomas Royden* (1837) and were reconstituted as the Egremont Steam Packet Company in 1838. Nevertheless, the service remained just as unreliable as in Askew's time and the company was wound-up in 1845. The ferry passed to John Sothern, who in turn sold it on in 1847 to John Fletcher for around £19,000. In May 1848, Fletcher leased the ferry to the Coulborn brothers who ran New Brighton ferry and then sold it to them on 1 September 1849 for the same price he had paid for it. The Coulborns established their headquarters at Egremont and between 1850 and 1856 spent £5,500 on improving the landing stage. The pier was extended to 238ft and a run out stage extending to 798ft on rails was provided along the stone slipway.

On 1 August 1861, all three Wallasey ferries passed into the hands of Wallasey Corporation and a survey carried out in 1871 showed that the Egremont Pier of the 1850s was already in a poor condition and needed replacing. The pier was closed on 12 January 1874 to allow work to start on a new structure designed by William Carson. This was to feature a 280ft iron pier situated 35ft above the low water level, and a movable 370ft long extension stage running along the slipway underneath. Powered by a winding gear driven by a hydraulic engine, the stage was mounted on wheels which moved along three rails. A bowstring bridge connected the pier with a tripod dolphin that guided the extension. The new pier was opened on 25 March 1875 and ships could now call even at the lowest of tides. New offices, workshops and booking office were erected at the pier entrance and became the headquarters of Wallasey's ferry operations. In total the works cost £14,000.

The new pier soon met up with a mishap however when on 29 September 1875 the boiler in the hydraulic engine house exploded,

The Mersey ferry pier at Egremont pictured on a postcard in 1904 with the run-out landing stage in use for the visiting ferry boat. The iron pier was opened in 1875 to a length of 280ft and the run out stage could extend a further 375ft. Marlinova Collection

destroying the building and rendering the run-out stage immovable. The stage was out in the Mersey at the time and became derailed by the rising tide. The boiler was repaired (and a duplicate one added to avoid this problem again) as was the run-out stage, which was further improved in 1878. Following the death of a young boy who was crushed by the run-out stage, a man with a red flag was used to warn when the stage was to be used. A proposal in 1888 to further extend the pier and slipway was rejected, although a much-needed waiting room was added at the end of the pier.

During the 1890s Egremont was linked to New Brighton by a fine 45ft wide promenade. Mother Redcap's Café, a legendary haunt of wreckers, smugglers, excise men and press gangs with its secret passages and caves, was an attraction along the promenade for visitors.[7] A notable landmark was the 13ft high clock tower of the Liverpool Home for Aged Mariners, built in 1882. Whilst waiting for the ferry, passengers could refresh themselves at the Egremont Ferry Hotel.

On 29 September 1897, the pier was damaged during a storm. The structure was repaired but was further damaged in a gale the following year and was in need of a full refurbishment or replacement. Although the ferry was a loss maker, the council continued to keep it open and

In 1909 Egremont Pier was extended to 815ft and it is seen here during the 1930s. The extension can clearly be defined by the lack of bracing on the supporting piles. The pier was demolished after it was damaged by ship collision in May 1941. Marlinova Collection

in February 1908 they decided it should be refurbished and extended. The engineer John James Webster decided to extend the pier to 815ft in length and add a floating landing stage to be set at right angles to the pier (allowing the run-out stage to be abandoned). Alex Findlay & Co of Motherwell was awarded the contract to carry out the work at a cost of £13,310 and commenced work on 2 February 1909. However, just a couple of weeks into the work, on 19 February, the partially dismantled tripod collapsed killing a foreman and injuring three workers. The ferry buildings were also entirely reconstructed and the new pier was opened on 8 November 1909. A saloon and bandstand were added at the ferry's entrance in 1912. A claim by LE Ford in 1912 that the new pier was unsafe was strenuously denied by Wallasey Corporation.

In 1929, the floating stage was reconstructed and the bridge leading to it widened by 3ft. However, on 21 May 1932, the pier was extensively damaged when it was rammed by the large oil tanker *British Commander*: 290ft of the pier collapsed and the bridge connecting the pier with the landing stage lay on its inshore end at the bottom of the river. Plans were drawn up by Sir John Wolfe Barry and Partners to repair the pier at a cost of £7,430 and it was back in service on 1 August 1933. However, following the opening of the road tunnel under the Mersey in 1934

Wallasey Corporation attempted to close Egremont Ferry because of declining passenger numbers. Local pressure kept the service running, but following another collision, by the *Newlands* on 13 May 1941, the pier was closed for good and its demolition was completed by August 1946. The stone slipway had been removed by 1948 at a cost of £3,000 by the Demolition and Construction Company.

The entrance buildings to the pier remained in situ, but were eventually demolished in the 1980s and the site is now an open promenade. Opposite, the Egremont Ferry pub remains open. The former ferry landing stage is now used as a floating HQ for the Island Cruising Club in Salcombe, South Devon,

SEACOMBE

The earliest reference to a ferry in the Seacombe area is recorded in the Domesday Book of 1086 and during the fourteenth century nearby Tokesford (present day Poulton Bridge) was used for sailings across Wallasey Pool and over to Liverpool. By 1541, Seacombe Ferry had been sold to the Crown, who leased it at an annual rent of 9s 8d to William Bromley. However, within two years Bromley had transferred the lease to John Minshull, the Lord of Tranmere, who established a rival ferry to Woodside at Tranmere. By 1586 though, when John Poole had taken over the running of the two ferries, Seacombe was described as being decayed. It was nevertheless soon brought back into service and during the seventeenth century it was used to ship horses to a race course near Wallasey village.

In 1797, whilst under the ownership of Rear Admiral Richard Smith, the ferry cost 2d for market people and 6d for the 'upper order of people'. Following Smith's death in 1811, his son, also named Richard, took over the ferry. He re-sited the terminal and built an earth and stone slipway in about 1815. Smith's trustees leased out the ferry to Stanley Garner, proprietor of the nearby Stanley Hotel, one of a number of hostelries springing up in the area to cater for visitors from Liverpool. In 1819, Thomas Parry opened the Seacombe Hotel directly opposite the ferry slip and this soon acquired a fine reputation for the excellence of its cuisine and fine gardens. Parry took over the running of the ferry that year and introduced the steamer *Seacombe* in 1822, followed by the *Alice* and *Alexander* in 1824. An hourly service was advertised with a single fare of 3d and this was regulated by the clock on the front of the hotel and a warning bell which rang two minutes before each departure.

A small dry dock was built in 1826 to assist in the maintenance of Parry's fleet, but landing facilities remained far from perfect and the foundation for a new slipway was laid on 5 June 1835. The new slipway had an incline of 1 in 20 and included a wooden extension on rails powered by a stationary winding engine. It was opened in the spring of 1836 and a half-hourly service was advertised, still at the rate of 3d. The old slipway of 1815 was used for landing coal and other goods.

In 1847, Thomas Parry's sons John and Richard inherited the ferry and during the next five years they acquired three second-hand ferries to replace their aging craft. However, in line with the reduction of the fares on the Woodside and Tranmere ferries to 1d, Seacombe had followed suit by 1853. With very little profit to be made from their enterprises, the Parry brothers decided to sell the hotel and give up the lease of the ferry and sell their steamers. Thomas Prestopino acquired the ferry lease for one year in March 1853 and operated it using the former Parry steamers *Britannia, Invincible* and *Thomas Wilson*. However, his brief tenure proved to be disastrous and in March 1854 the Coulborn brothers Edward and William, who ran the ferries at Egremont and New Brighton, took the lease on a year-to-year basis. They oversaw the reconstruction of the landing stage after the run out stage was badly damaged by ice during the winter of 1854–5. The stone slipway was increased to a length of 540ft and a new run out stage of 180ft was laid on a track of three rails, which was opened for use in early 1857.

The Coulborns soon turned around the fortunes of Seacombe by integrating its ferries with those for Egremont and New Brighton. A simple fare structure was adopted to cross the Mersey: 1d from Seacombe, 2d from Egremont and 3d from New Brighton and there were also services between the three places. All three Wallasey ferries passed to the Local Board on 1 August 1861, the rights of passage for Seacombe Ferry being acquired from the Smith's Trustees for around £30,000. Between 1876 and 1880, Wallasey Corporation rebuilt the landing stage at Seacombe in conjunction with the reclaiming of Seacombe Bay. William Carson was appointed engineer and work began in May 1876. From the following July all sailings were transferred to the landing stage and 150ft connecting bridge salvaged from the failed Liverpool South End stage at Toxteth, which had been acquired as a temporary landing stage. The new Seacombe landing stage was 310ft long and came complete with passenger and goods bridges (built by Thomas Brassey and Company at Birkenhead), a hydraulic lift for vehicular traffic and a machinery building incorporating a clock tower at the entrance. It was officially opened on 5 January 1880 having cost a total of £143,000 to build and in October of that year a rail connection was laid from the ferry to the Dock Board line in Birkenhead Road. Meanwhile, a new Seacombe Ferry Hotel had been opened adjoining the ferry in 1876, which boasted its own pleasure grounds for visitors.[8]

Whilst the new landing stage was being built, one of the paddle steamers operating from Seacombe *Gem* collided with the *Bowfell*, a wooden paddle steamer at anchor in the river, on 26 November 1878 causing the loss of five lives. Three new steamers for the crossing were under construction at the time; the passenger vessels *Daisy* and *Primrose* and the luggage vessel *Sunflower*, and they were brought into service the following year. *Sunflower's* time as a goods vessel was brief however, for in 1882 she was converted for passenger use and a further ship *Violet* was brought into use in 1883. The paddle steamer *Thistle* and luggage boat *Shamrock* (ex-Birkenhead Woodside) joined the fleet in 1891, joined four years later by the paddle steamers *Pansy* and *John Herron* and the coal barge *Emily*. In 1900 two twin-screw steamers, called *Rose* and *Lily* were built on the Mersey for the ferry service and in the following year the double twin-screw luggage boat *Seacombe* was built by Cochran of Annan at a cost of £18,000. An extension of the Wirral Railway to Seacombe was authorised in 1893 and through tickets on the railway and ferry were made available, as they were when the Dee & Birkenhead Railway from Wrexham was granted running powers over the Wirral Line from Bidston to Seacombe in 1898. Competition for the railways to Seacombe was provided from May 1902 by the electric trams that connected Seacombe with New Brighton on three different routes.

On 24 March 1898, the Seacombe landing stage was seriously damaged after the SS *Lake Winnipeg* ran into the *Wallasey* and *Thistle* that were moored there. One of the hydraulic gangways collapsed onto the stage and both good lifts were put out of action. It took several weeks of repairs before the landing stage was fit for use again. Seacombe suffered a further calamity on 12 February 1909, when the Dominion liner *Octopus* caused severe damage to the landing stage after crashing into it whilst trying to avoid a pacific liner. A happier event was the landing of King George V and Queen Mary on 25 March 1914 to lay the foundation stone for the new town hall.

During the First World War four Wallasey Ferries – *Pansy, John Herron, Iris* and *Daffodil* were requisitioned for war service, although *Pansy* was wrecked on the Anglesey coast on 21 January 1917, just a day after she left the Mersey. *Iris* and *Daffodil* took part in the famous Zeebrugge naval raid on 23 April 1918 and were subsequently honoured with Royal prefixes.

Business was maintained at Seacombe to impressive levels both during the war and after: in 1919 alone, 22 million passengers used the ferry. However, the stage was showing its age and plans were made for its total replacement. Work began in 1924 and on 23 October 1926 a new Seacombe landing stage costing £206,000 was opened by Lord

A picture postcard of the Seacombe landing stage posted on 31 December 1904. Opened in 1880, the entrance building to the stage had a clock tower, seen on the right of the card. Marlinova Collection

Derby. The replacement landing stage consisted of a 485ft floating stage that could accommodate three boats, a three-track floating roadway for vehicular traffic and the existing passenger bridges. To compliment the new stage, an impressive new terminal building with a distinctive new clock tower was opened on 10 April 1933 at a cost of £98,443.[9]

Around 10,000 passengers per hour could use the new stage and boats sailed every fifteen minutes. In 1932 the vessel *Royal Iris II* was introduced by Wallasey, followed by the *Royal Daffodil II* in 1934. However the opening of the Queensway Mersey Road Tunnel in 1934 drastically reduced the vehicular traffic sailing from Seacombe. The ferry lost an estimated two million passengers and by the 1940s the luggage boats had ceased.

Nevertheless, Wallasey continued to introduce new vessels, diesel powered rather than paddle steamers, on to their two remaining routes (Seacombe and New Brighton). The third *Royal Iris* was delivered in 1951: she was the largest vessel built for the Mersey service and could carry up to 2,296 passengers. In addition to her ferry duties, she was also used as a popular day cruise ship and was nicknamed the 'love boat', 'booze boat' and 'fish and chip boat'.[10] The 1950s also saw the introduction of the *Leasowe* (1951), *Egremont* (1952) and *Royal Daffodil III* (1958).

However, falling passenger numbers using Seacombe led to economies being carried out to the landing stage. In May 1956, the removal of

The latest version of the Seacombe Mersey Ferry landing stage, built in 2000 and photographed here in October 2008. Marlinova Collection

the largely redundant floating roadway was commenced, which was completed by February 1957. The floating landing stage was then shortened by 150ft in 1964–6 at a cost of £37,597.

The Seacombe and Woodside ferries passed to the Merseyside Passenger Transport Executive on 1 December 1969 and an extra gangway was built to enable the former Birkenhead boats to use Seacombe. Despite a threat of closure during the 1970s Seacombe remains open and seemingly has an assured future as one of the three landing stages for the Mersey Ferries River Explorer Cruises. A new landing stage was opened in 2000, and four years later Merseytravel opened the Spaceport attraction at Seacombe at a cost of £9 million which features a 360° Space Dome Planetarium. In addition, the terminal also has a café, children's play area and souvenir shop. A display on the Zeebrugge Raid on German U-boats in 1918, in which the Mersey ferries *Iris* and *Daffodil* took part, is planned for Seacombe to complement the placing of U-boat U-534 at Woodside.

BIRKENHEAD WOODSIDE

Woodside Ferry is the longest surviving of the Birkenhead chain of ferry landing stages. Under a charter granted by King Edward III, rights included the provision to the Prior of Birkenhead of a ferry service between Birkenhead and Liverpool. The priory had been established in 1150 and the monks rowed passengers across the river for a small fee when the weather was fine. The river was wider then and passengers had to be landed on the Pool on the north side of the river (near to the present site of the Merseyside Police Headquarters). A royal licence was granted in 1317 to enable the priory to build houses lodging people crossing the river and in 1330 Edward III granted *the right of ferry there ... for men, horses and goods, with leave to charge reasonable tolls.*

Following the dissolution of the monasteries the ferry rights passed to the crown, who sold them along with the priory properties to Sir Ralph Worsley in 1544 for £586 11s 6d. The ferry was then operated by Sir Thomas Powell before being purchased by Alderman John Cleveland of Liverpool. Following Cleveland's death, the ferry rights passed by inheritance to Francis Richard Price. By 1818, Price leased the rights of the Woodside ferry to William Woods, who placed the following advertisement in Gore's *Liverpool Directory* that year:

WOODSIDE ROYAL FERRY, Royal Chester and Holyhead Mail Coach 4p.m. Chester and Shrewsbury Commercial Coach, 8.45 a.m. to Chester, via Sutton, through Wrexham, Overton, Ellesmere, to Shrewsbury, at which place it is met by coaches to Oswestry, Welshpool, &c., and all parts of South Wales. Returns every day at 4 o'clock.

In 1822, Woods passed the rights to a local innkeeper, Hugh Williams. Price extended the size of the ferry hotel and built a 30ft slipway in time for Williams to commence a service to Liverpool using the paddle steamer *Royal Mail*. The *Frances* was used in 1825 followed by *Hercules* (1828), *St David* (1828), *Kingfisher* (1830), *Ribble* (1832), *Ann* (1834) and *Enterprise* (1834). In 1835, the lease was transferred to the Woodside, North Birkenhead & Liverpool Steam Ferry Company, formed by local businessmen to improve the service, who rebuilt the slipway as a stone pier. The company's steamer *Helensburgh* did the trip to Liverpool in only five minutes. The *Cleveland* and *Eliza Price* were added to the service in 1836 and other vessels that operated the service included *Nun* (1840), *Tobermory* (1841), *Queen* (1841), *Prince* (1844), *Wirral* (1846), *Lord Morpeth* (1847), *Woodside* (1853), *Liverpool* (1855), *Newport* (1860), *Cheshire* (1863), *Lancashire* (1865), *Woodside II* (1865) and *Claughton* (1876). A luggage boat service was started in 1879 which ran until 1939.

The rights to operate a ferry from Birkenhead Woodside date back to the twelfth century and it remains the only Birkenhead ferry in operation today. This postcard shows it in c.1910 as seen from the river. Marlinova Collection

In 1842, the ownership of the Woodside Ferry was due to pass from Francis Price and the Birkenhead & Chester Railway Company (who held the majority of the shares) to the Birkenhead Commissioners (from 1877 Birkenhead Corporation). The deal fell through however, although the ferry was leased to the commissioners until they eventually purchased the operation in 1858. In 1862, the Corporation opened a new floating landing stage on reclaimed land between the Woodside Hotel and the old pier. The pontoons were moored by chains originally made for the SS *Great Eastern* and two bridges linked the pontoon with the shore. An arched glazed roof was added for customer's protection in 1863. The following year saw the *Cheshire*, the first passenger ferry steamer to have a saloon, operate from Woodside.

The opening of the first section of the Mersey Railway between Green Lane, Birkenhead and James Street, Liverpool on 1 February 1886 saw a decline in numbers using Woodside from 12.04 million to 5.26 in 1889–90. However, there was a slight revival of passenger numbers during the 1890s that reached 7.98 million by 1897–8 during the period when twin-screw passenger steamers were replacing the paddle steamers. *Lancashire* and *Claughton II* entered service in 1899, followed by *Bidston* and *Woodside III* in 1903. Passenger figures using Woodside were also boosted with the electrification in 1901–2 of the Birkenhead Tramways running to the ferry. The electrification of the Mersey Railway on 3 May 1903 speeded up rail travel between Birkenhead and Liverpool to just eight minutes, although this failed to greatly affect the ratios travelling on the railway and ferries which remained around 60% rail to 40% ferries. In 1912 10.2 million passengers were using Woodside, almost double that of twenty years earlier and road, cattle and luggage traffic using the crossing was increasing fast. By 1920 this had led to serious congestion on the approaches to the goods ferries on both sides of the river, and vehicular ferry services were in dire need of updating. Work on a new berth and floating roadway was undertaken at Woodside, which was completed in February 1921, but traffic congestion leading back from the ferry terminal remained a problem. Two new goods boats, *Barnston* and *Churton*, entered service in October and November 1921. These were joined in 1925 by two further goods ferries (*Bebington* and *Oxton*) and two passenger vessels, ordered from Cammel Laird at a cost of £220,000. One of the passenger vessels *Upton* was used on the Rock Ferry service whilst the other *Hinderton* was for Woodside. The ordinary fare on the ferry had been reduced to 2d and a range of tram/bus and ferry tickets had been introduced to combat competition from the Mersey Railway. The year 1926–7 proved to be a prosperous one for Woodside with over 14 million passengers using it, and this level was to be only slightly reduced in the succeeding years. However, major work had to be carried out to the landing stage after it was rammed by a coaster in 1928. Road traffic continued to rise and more than a million vehicles crossed the river via Woodside in 1930. In that year, two further steamers were added to the Birkenhead fleet: *Claughton III* and *Thurstaston*, replacing the 1899 pair *Lancashire* and *Claughton II*. They were joined in 1933 by *Bidston II*, built to replace its namesake of 1903 which was sold to Blackpool Pleasure Steamers Ltd and became *Minden*.

However, the opening of the Mersey road tunnel in 1934 saw almost all vehicular goods traffic transferred from Woodside to the tunnel and car traffic also began to desert the ferries, although bus services were not allowed to use the tunnel.[11] Further patronage was lost by the ferries when the Wirral lines of the LMS Railway were electrified from 14 March 1938 and through services from West Kirby and New Brighton were run over the Mersey Railway to Liverpool.

The passenger ferries continued to run during the Second World War, but on 21 July 1941 the goods service ceased, never to return. After being used to unload military aircraft during the war, *Bebington* and *Oxton* were sold for scrap in 1949.

Passenger numbers returned to around 11 million after the war, but the ferries were now losing money and the Mersey Tunnel Joint Committee were pressurising Birkenhead Corporation to make cutbacks in order to reduce an annual deficit of £50,000. The Tunnel Committee renewed its support for the ferries in 1955 but required the end of night ferries (to be replaced by buses through the tunnel) and a rise in the fares.[12] Woodside's floating roadway was closed that same year and was removed in 1958. In 1960 Birkenhead introduced the diesel-powered vessels *Mountwood* and *Woodchurch*, which were joined by the *Overchurch* two years later. These had accommodation for 1,200 passengers.

By the mid-1960s the landing stage was feeling its age, particularly the pontoons, a number of which needed replacing. A number of small improvements were carried out including a new screen between the passenger stage and the disused goods stage and in 1967 a new ticket office, but money was not available for any major work. This was left to the Merseyside Passenger Transport Executive who, under the provisions of the Transport Act 1968, acquired all public transport undertakings in Liverpool, Birkenhead and Wallasey on 1 December 1969. The new owners had to deal with declining passenger numbers and the full financial burden of running the ferries following the termination of the agreement with the Mersey Tunnel Joint Committee on 17 July 1974. Furthermore, the second Mersey Tunnel, serving Wallasey, was opened on 28 June 1971. Passenger numbers using the Woodside and Seacombe ferries had fallen to less than 5,000 a day and they were losing £800,000 a year. Closure of the ferry services was proposed by the MPTE, but in the face of public pressure the new Merseyside County Council voted to retain the ferries on a reduced level and they were saved in 1977.

Woodside landing stage photographed from a Mersey ferry in October 2008. The stage had been totally rebuilt in 1986 at a cost of £3.2m. Marlinova Collection

The operation of the ferries was finally combined in May 1981 when its administration was centred at Seacombe: this had been prompted by the destruction of the ferry workshops at Woodside in May 1980. The year 1984 proved to be a highpoint in the revival of the ferries. A service was provided to the Garden Festival at Otterspool using a new landing stage, and during the four-day Tall Ships Race in August some 250,000 passengers were carried.

Following a report by a team of marine consultants, the council decided in 1985 that the Woodside landing stage would have to be totally refurbished. A new stage, designed by Kingham Knights Associates and built by Die-Biesbosch in the Netherlands was opened on 13 March 1986 at a cost of £3.2 million. The new works featured a steel pontoon measuring 171ft x 79ft x 10ft 6in connected to the terminal building by a lattice girder passenger bridge. The listed Victorian waiting room of 1864 was refurbished and currently features a café.

The current fleet of the Mersey Ferries consists of the three ex-Birkenhead trio of *Royal Iris of the Mersey* (ex-*Mountwood*), *Snowdrop* (formerly *Woodchurch*) and *Royal Daffodil* (*Overchurch*). They provide an hourly summer triangular service between Liverpool, Seacombe and Woodside. In a bid to attract more tourist trade to the Woodside terminal, Merseytravel is to provide a new berth alongside the landing stage to house German U-boat U-534. The boat will be cut into three sections allowing visitors to see inside the submarine from specially built viewing platforms. The U-boat will be sited opposite a life-size model of *Resurgam*, one of the earliest submarines.

BIRKENHEAD MONKS FERRY

The Monks Ferry Company was formed by the Bryan family in 1837, who built a hotel and stone slipway 400 yards south of Woodside, on the site (they claimed) of the former priory crossing. Sailings commenced in April 1838 using the wooden paddle steamers *Monk* and *Abbey*, with an iron steamer named *Dolphin* added to the fleet in January 1840. However, the owner of Woodside Ferry entered into legal proceedings to have this rival service terminated and in February 1840 the Monks Ferry services were ordered to cease.

The assets of the Monks Ferry Company were sold to the Birkenhead and Chester Railway Company who held a majority in the Woodside Ferry. They reopened the service from Monks Ferry upon the opening of the railway on 23 September 1840, and a train service was commenced to Monks Ferry on 23 October 1844 to connect with the ferry services. The railway company maintained the times of the sailings even after the purchasing of Monks Ferry by Birkenhead Corporation for £20,000 on 31 May 1847. In addition to passenger traffic, the landing of soldiers and the Dublin mail was carried out at Monks Ferry. The corporation however found the ferry to be a white elephant due to the small amount of passenger traffic and high operating costs and were relieved when the ferry was transferred to the London & North Western and Great Western railway companies (who had jointly purchased the Chester-Birkenhead line) on 1 January 1862. However, as the railway company had no boats, the corporation lucratively supplied them for £100 per week. In 1864 the hire charge was raised to £112 per week and £120 from 1 July 1867 but when the corporation withdrew the boats the railway ordered three vessels *Thames*, *Mersey* and *Severn*. They commenced operations from Monks Ferry in June 1868.

The service from Monks Ferry was finally abandoned in 1878 upon the opening of a new railway station at Woodside. The *Thames*, *Mersey* and *Severn* were transferred elsewhere and the ferry site was adapted into a coal depot.

BIRKENHEAD

George La French of Tranmere Ferry opened a further ferry service at the northern edge of Tranmere Pool in 1820, next to the Birkenhead Hotel,

An engraving of Birkenhead Ferry by John Davies c.1830 with the Birkenhead Hotel seen in the background. The hotel was closed in 1850 and the ferry followed suit in 1870. Marlinova Collection

opened by William Mears the previous year. The provision of bathing and bowling facilities quickly led to the hotel becoming a fashionable meeting place. La French built a slipway and quay in 1822, but both the ferry and hotel passed first to James Ball, also involved at Tranmere Ferry, in 1827. A half- hourly service was provided to Parade Slip, Liverpool using the vessels *Abbey* from 1822 and *Vesuvius* from 1832, although the vessels owned by La French and Ball at Tranmere may also have operated the Birkenhead service.

In 1841, Birkenhead Ferry and Hotel were purchased by Liverpool Corporation for £73,800 with an eye to halt the expansion of Birkenhead Docks and build an extension of their docks on the Cheshire shore. They leased the ferry to Messrs Hetherington and Grindrod until 1846 before operating the service themselves as they were unable to find a lessee. In 1848 the iron paddle steamer *Fanny* was introduced onto the route and the ferry was reduced to 1d, yet it was annually losing £5,000–£6,000 and could not compete with Woodside. Nevertheless, two further steamers, *Cato* and *Vernon* (both named after their respective builders Cato, Miller and Company and T Vernon), were introduced in 1849. They were only to run under the corporation's banner for two years before, along with *Fanny*, they were acquired by the Willoughbys, the operators of Tranmere Ferry, who had leased the ferry from 15 February 1851 for fourteen years. The Birkenhead Hotel however was not taken over, having closed the previous year along with coach service to Parkgate.

One of the Willoughby's first acts at Birkenhead was to build a long bridge across Tranmere Pool to Tranmere Ferry to enable both their ferries to be used by one set of ships. However its remoteness from public transport was ensuring that Birkenhead Ferry was in terminal decline. On 9 August 1870, it was offered at auction on a 999 year lease but remained unsold and was closed. Two years later the ferry site was acquired by Lairds for an extension to their shipyard, although the hotel survived until 1904.

TRANMERE

A ferry is known to have operated from Tranmere since at least 1552 when John Minshull, the Lord of Tranmere and also owner of Seacombe Ferry, established a crossing in opposition to Woodside. In 1586, Elizabeth I granted John Poole of Sutton the right to operate the Tranmere service, although Seacombe Ferry was described at the time as 'decayed'. W Roberts was operating Tranmere by the early 1800s and there was a connecting coach from the ferry to Chester, Wrexham and Chirk, where it met the coaches to Shrewsbury and Holyhead. On 31 January 1812 the *Liverpool Mercury* announced the letting of Tranmere Ferry and Hotel:

TRANMERE FERRY AND HOTEL – TO BE LET – All that capital and well accustomed INN and FERRY HOUSE, comprising 4 parlours, 2 tea rooms and 12 bedrooms, good stabling, 2 coach-houses, five cellars & c. together with the privilege of the QUAY, now going to be extended 400 yards, on a high level above water mark; and also 30 or 40 acres of LAND in a ring fence.

The situation of this Ferry, only 1 mile from Liverpool opposite to the New Docks, the constant passage of boats every half hour across the river, the convenience of sea bathing, machine, &c. with the healthy situations and beautiful views of Liverpool, the Docks, Hoylake, the Sea, Birkenhead Abbey, the Woods, &c. render this situation one of the best and most desirable on the River Mersey. N.B. Two or three coaches run daily between Chester and Liverpool by Tranmere Ferry.

A large new HOUSE, containing four parlours and 18 bedrooms, with a walled garden and 10 acres of land, distant 200yds, may be taken with or without the Ferry, suitable for a genteel Family, or bathing Hotel, with Stable and Coach House.

Most eligible lots of land for Marine Villas may be had near the said premises, at Holt Hill and in Hinderton Lane.

Apply (if by letter, post paid) to Mr Faulkner, Attorney at Law, Chester.

The extension of the quay with a ferry landing slipway mentioned in the advertisement came to fruition on 4 April 1817. William Bateman and George La French introduced the wooden paddle steamer *Etna* (or *Aetna*) on the ferry at the same time, which ran to Queens Dock in Liverpool. At the same time, James Ball ran the *Regulator* from Tranmere to the Parade Slip in Liverpool. Ball was also involved in the Birkenhead Ferry, established in 1820. In 1838, William Willoughby and son acquired the ferry, but it was declining in popularity due to the opening of the Birkenhead and Chester Railway and improvements at Woodside. The Willoughbys closed the ferry for a time during the 1840s, although they reopened it in 1848. Three years later they took over the lease of the Birkenhead Ferry and ran both ferries using a wooden bridge laid across Tranmere Pool.

The Willoughbys continued to operate Tranmere Ferry until the expiration of their lease on 29 June 1872. Samuel Davies acquired the ferry rights and formed the Tranmere Ferry Company, which was incorporated on 31 January 1873 with a capital of £25,000. Davies was the major shareholder amongst the local businessmen involved in the company, as he was in the associated Tranmere Shipping Company. The ferry was reopened in May 1873 using the vessels *Lord Morpeth* and *Superb*.

Negotiations were held with the Rock Ferry Company between 1874 and 1876 with the intention of running the two ferries as one operation,

and stageman's shelter. The landing stage, constructed of wrought iron kelsons and greenheart decking, floated on ten pontoons and was secured by six anchors. At the entrance to the pier a large red brick tollhouse surmounted by a clock tower was provided. On 30 June 1899, the pier was formally opened by the Mayor of Birkenhead, JT Thompson Esq having cost a total of £18,602 to construct. The official party sailed from the pier to Liverpool aboard the *Mersey* and upon their return the pier was officially opened to the public whilst the dignitaries dined at the Royal Rock Hotel. The day's festivities were concluded with fireworks provided by Pains of London.

The passenger numbers using Rock Ferry and New Ferry however failed to come up to expectations. Both piers were rather remote from public transport and many people preferred to catch the ferry at Woodside, which was connected to New Ferry by an electric tramway opened on 4 February 1901. The numbers using Rock Ferry did pick up however in 1903 following a reduction of the fare to Liverpool from 2d to 1d and then stabilised at around 1.8million each year till the end of the decade. Nevertheless a loss of around £4,000 was incurred annually on the passenger traffic and the pier itself often required maintenance, such as when the landing stage dragged its anchor on Good Friday 1904.

Rock Ferry Pier and floating landing stage photographed c.1920 with the old slipway seen alongside. The pier was 780ft long and opened in 1899 at a cost of £18,602. Marlinova Collection

An attraction for visitors to Rock Ferry were the three wooden ships, *Conway, Akbar* and *Indefatigable,* moored in the Mersey for use as training and reformatory vessels. Rock Ferry Pier was often used as a landing stage for those going to and from the vessels. Boys from the vessels were frequent visitors to the Olympian Gardens, which by 1910 were being leased by the concert party entrepreneurs Adeler, Sutton and Allendale. During the season they presented a daily fare of around eight vaudeville entertainers (changed weekly), principally consisting of singers and comedians. Seat prices ranged from 9d at the front, 6d in the second row and 3d at the back and on the promenade. In August 1910, the gardens were being presented as the Winter Gardens (late Olympian Gardens) *the ideal summer evening resort* with evening shows commencing at 8p.m. and an afternoon matinee on Mondays. The gardens remained a feature of Rock Ferry until they were closed in 1925.

During the 1920s, passengers using Rock Ferry remained at a respectable level, although its operation continued to lose money for Birkenhead Corporation. Extra bus services were laid on to the pier,

Rock Ferry Pier photographed from the old slipway in October 2008. Closed as a ferry pier in 1939, it has been used since 1957 in connection with an oil refinery, who added the jetty at the end of the pier. Marlinova Collection

including one to Port Sunlight from 12 March 1921. This proved popular with visitors from Liverpool to the Lever Brothers soap works as the quickest way to the works was by the ferry to Rock Ferry and then the connecting bus. Bank holidays and high summer often saw heavy patronage of the pier, particularly by cyclists: in 1924 over the Easter holiday 43,366 passengers used the ferry service. However, operating losses continued to mount, averaging £13,700 annually in 1922–7 and the corporation, having successfully closed New Ferry, began contemplating whether Rock Ferry should go as well. Nevertheless, in 1925, a new ferry, *Upton,* was built for the Rock Ferry Service (joining *Storeton,* introduced in 1910), and in the following year the pier decking was renewed at a cost of £1,793.

By the mid-1930s, average daily passenger use of the pier was around 3,000, which was bolstered by heavy seasonal weekend traffic. Closure was now being seriously considered, and despite a proposal to run just a summer only service, the final sailing from Rock Ferry Pier was undertaken by *Upton* on 30 June 1939.

Storeton was sold to the Leith Salvage and Towing Company for £2,375 on 28 May 1940, and following wartime service with the Ministry of Transport, *Upton* went down south in April 1946 having been sold to the Southampton, Isle of Wight and South of England Royal Mail Steam Packet Company for £15,000. Rock Ferry Pier meanwhile narrowly avoided being demolished for scrap metal during the war and appears to have been used for some wartime service. In November 1951, an agreement was reached for the staff of Bromborough Tanker Moorings to use the pier until it was sold by Birkenhead Corporation to Cammel Laird for £2,500 on 29 March 1956, who intended to use it for oil tanker cleaning purposes. In March 1957, they removed the bridge and floating landing stage and added a 600ft jetty facing north-east from the end of the pier. At the end of the new jetty was a platform of 275ft with two main berthing dolphins and six separate mooring dolphins and the alterations were completed in 1959.

The pier remains in situ today, as does the slipway, although sadly the area around them has become very run down. The Royal Rock Hotel was demolished in the 1960s, the old pier terminal building has also gone and the esplanade has been left to crumble away. A visit to the area in October 2008 saw the Admiral pub (formerly the Refreshment Rooms) closed and the buildings around the former pier entrance very run down. The A41 Rock Ferry bypass has sliced through the elegant villas of Rock Park (now Grade II listed), necessitating the demolition of some of them (including Nathaniel Hawthorne's villa), and cut off the attractive Mersey Yacht Club and esplanade area from the rest of the town.

New Ferry

Situated in the parish of Bebington, the commencement of a 'new ferry' from here to Liverpool in 1774, gave its name to the district surrounding the ferry which has endured to the present day, long after the ferry was closed. A slipway *extending into the River Mersey for a long distance below the high water mark* provided landing facilities and the ferry was connected to Chester by coach.

On 2 July 1857, by order of the Trustees of the late William Charles Lake, an auction was held of freehold and leasehold property at New Ferry, which included a hotel and large garden, 'pier' and coal wharf. In 1861, Robert Macfie, a wealthy sugar merchant residing at Neston Hall, expressed an interest in erecting a pier at New Ferry. In September 1863 he inaugurated the formation of the Mersey River Steam Boat Company with a capital of £20,000 in £5 shares to operate a triangular ferry service between New Ferry, Liverpool Pier Head (Princes Dock) and Liverpool South End (Toxteth). The pier site at New Ferry, which adjoined the slipway, was leased from the Office of Woods for a period of eighty years at a yearly rent of £20 and the formal ferry rights were acquired on 23 October 1865. The eminent Scottish engineer James Brunlees was engaged to erect an iron pier, which was to be 856ft in length (Brunlees used the same design for the ferry pier at New Brighton). The contractors W&J Galloway of Manchester (who had worked with Brunlees at Southport Pier in 1859–60) began work in 1864 and the pier was opened the on 4 April 1865 at a cost of £11,477. A floating landing stage was also erected at Liverpool South End and the service between New Ferry and Liverpool commenced in 1865 with two trips every hour. The steamers *Sprite* and *Sylph II* were acquired for the route, with the *Syren* being added in December 1865.

The opening of the pier was reported in the *Illustrated London News* on 29 April 1865:

A new ferry across the Mersey, between Toxteth Park, Liverpool, and the opposite part of the Cheshire shore, which is henceforth to be called 'New Ferry', has been established by the Mersey River Steamboat Company (Limited), and was opened for traffic by the Mayor of Liverpool on Monday, the 4th inst. The works at each end of the ferry are worthy of some notice. On the Liverpool side of the Mersey the permanent structure belonging to the Mersey River Steamboat Company consists of a floating landing-stage, which measures 120ft in length and 30ft in breadth. The stage is securely moored in the river by strong mooring chains a short distance seaward of the Harrington Dock wall, with which it is connected by a well-constructed wrought-iron bridge 150ft in length, and which weighs about sixty tons. The stage, the deck of which is supported on a pontoon made of wrought iron, which rises and falls with the tide, was constructed by Messrs Bowdler, Chaffers & Co., iron ship builders of Seacombe. The bridge, which is in every respect convenient and highly serviceable, was made by Messrs Grayson and Son, Liverpool, from designs by and under the superintendence of Mr Douglas Hebson, engineer of that town; both structures and their concomitants being admirably suited to the purposes of an extensive ferry business, and fully provided with lights and other conveniences. The pier or landing stage on the Cheshire side of the Mersey, at New Ferry, which is at once elegant and commodious, has been constructed from the designs of Mr James Brunlees, of Victoria Street, Westminster, who has most successfully carried out works of a similar character at Morecambe Bay, in viaducts on the line of the Ulverston and Lancaster Railway, and is now about to construct a railway viaduct across the Solway Firth on the same principle. The piers now about to be erected at New Brighton and Rhyl are also from designs by the same engineer. The New Ferry Pier commences from the land end with three rows of wrought-iron lattice-girders, 60ft in length and 4ft 6in in depth, supported by cast iron columns, of 12in external diameter, securely braced with angle irons; the platform, of four-inch planking, being laid on the bottom flange of the girders, which thus forms a substantial parapet. A centre girder divides the whole width of the roadway into two, each of which is 9ft wide. The pier proper is 850ft in length, consisting of fourteen bays or spans, each 60ft in length. At the end of this is a cluster of piles to form a steadying point of attachment for the top of the moveable bridge, the end of which is connected with a floating pontoon by suspension-chains hanging from a wrought-iron frame. The bridge itself is 158ft long and 9ft wide. The pontoon forming the landing stage is 100ft long and 22ft wide, and is moored up and down the river by four 1½ inch mooring-chains, which can be controlled by proper gearing on the deck. This elegant fabric, in which lightness of structure has been skilfully combined with strength, was erected by Messrs William Galloway & Sons, of Manchester, under the management of Mr H Hooper, who, as resident manager, superintended and carried out the work. The pier and its landing-stage have been erected at the sole expense of Mr R.A. Macfie.

The dejeuner provided to celebrate the opening was laid out in a large marquee pitched close to the pier. Mr Macfie and Messrs Galloway & Sons bore the expense of the entertainment. The company was very numerous, and included a number of ladies. Mr Macfie occupied the chair, Mr Matthew Gregson (the chairman of the board of directors) taking the vice-chair. Among the guests were his Worship the Mayor of Liverpool, Mr E. Lawrence, and many other gentlemen of local influence. In the evening the landing stage was brilliantly illuminated.

Despite the New Ferry Hotel and Gardens being situated close to the pier and attracting some visitors, the ferry service failed to flourish. In 1867, the ferry and steamers were acquired by Henry Gough of Eastham Ferry. He sold *Syren* and mortgaged *Sprite* and *Sylph II* to Robert Macfie. Gough died in 1871 and his business was run by Thomas Thompson, who carried on operating steamers from New Ferry using the steamers *Wasp*, *Fairy Queen* and *Gipsy Queen* until the landing stage[15] was carried away during a severe gale on 20 May 1887. Following renovation to the stage at a cost of £2,134 Macfie operated a triangular service between New Ferry, Rock Ferry and Liverpool from 1889 to 1891 until he closed Rock Ferry. New Ferry continued to have an hourly service using the SS *Firefly* until 1897 when Birkenhead Corporation took over the rights of New Ferry Pier for a period of thirty years and following the erection of a pier at Rock Ferry re-introduced the triangular service.

New Ferry attracted some visitors to a small area of beach called The Gap, although this later became lost. In 1907, Birkenhead Corporation proposed renewing the worn-out landing stage, which was carried out four years later by the Ailsa Shipbuilding Company at a cost of £5,587. The pier itself also received attention with the introduction of electric lighting and glass windscreens.

A postcard issued by Valentines showing the New Ferry Pier c.1910. The pier had been erected in 1865 to a length of 856ft. Note the advertisements and weighing machine at the front of the pier. Marlinova Collection

On the morning of 30 January 1922, four spans of the sea end of the pier was destroyed by the Dutch steamer *Stad Vlaardingen* during thick fog, ending the ferry service. Birkenhead Corporation were in no rush to reinstate it, claiming that the ferry service annually lost £20,000 and was very little used except in during the summer. They stated that upon the expiration in 1927 of their obligation under the 1897 act to operate the ferry they were not going to renew it. Therefore why should they carry out expensive repairs when the pier was to close in five years? Opposition to the closure was led by a 'Ferry Service Committee' and Bromborough and Bebington UDC but nevertheless a repeal of the obligation to maintain the ferry was implemented under the Birkenhead Corporation (Ferries) Act 1924. Demolition of the pier commenced almost immediately, undertaken by Arthur Wilkinson of Liverpool who had submitted a tender of £405. The ferry however was not officially closed until 22 September 1927 when the corporation's obligation to run it had officially expired. The pier entrance buildings and surrounding area were conveyed to Birkenhead Corporation for £100 in 1926.

A car park stands on the site of the shore end buildings and upon close inspection small pieces of iron show where the pier met the shore.

A look along New Ferry Pier to the shore c.1914 with the New Ferry Hotel looming large in the distance. The pier was last used in 1922 and demolished and the hotel is also no more although the terrace of houses on the left still survives. The boy in the foreground looks quite smart in his sailor suit. Marlinova Collection

EASTHAM

Eastham was the most southerly of the ten ferry landing stages on the western bank of the River Mersey, and records of a ferry at Eastham date back to 1357 when Edward the Black Prince granted a licence to the Poole family to operate a ferry. Eight years later it was recorded that four ferry boats operated without a licence from Bromborough and Eastham. Poole's licence passed to the monks of St Werburgh Abbey, Chester, who were said to have used the jetty to receive agricultural produce from Chester, north Wales and the south Wirral area. This became known as Job's Ferry or Carlett Ferry and the remains of the earth jetty could be seen 300 yards north of the later ferry terminal.

In 1707, Nicholas Blundell on a journey from Liverpool to Chester mentions an 'Eastham ferry boat'. By the 1780s a regular service was operating from Eastham to Liverpool using two very large, commodious and stout boats leaving the Dry Dock, Liverpool every two hours before high water from Eastham from whence a stagecoach carries passengers, parcels & c. to Chester fare by the coach, inside 3s 6d, 1s 9d outside.

A 1795 advertisement announced:

> A very complete decked boat sails from Mrs Urmston's Salthouse Dock Gates, to Eastham where it meets the Chester coach, capable of holding 16 persons. The coach leaves Chester about two hours before high water, with passengers for Liverpool and returns one hour after high water with passengers from Liverpool to Chester & c. Fare by the boat; first class 1s, second class 6d. Fare by the coach 3s 6d.

The early years of the nineteenth century saw Samuel Smith operating the Eastham Ferry and on 26 July 1816 the *Liverpool Daily Courier* reported:

> NEW STEAM PACKET TO EASTHAM. The 'Princess Charlotte' Steam Packet will sail from this port on Friday morning at eleven o'clock and return the same evening; on Saturday morning she will sail at eight o'clock and depart from Eastham at nine o'clock. She will sail again from the port at half past three o'clock in the afternoon and will meet the Chester coach. Places to be taken at Mr Thomas Dod's, James Street, Liverpool and at the White Lion, Chester; fares to Chester 3s inside, 2s outside.

The *Princess Charlotte* was still operating three years later, as recorded by the *Liverpool Directory*:

> The 'Princess Charlotte' (Steam) Packet sails to Eastham every morning at 8 and every afternoon at 3 (during spring, summer and autumn months)

from the Parade, west side of St George's Dock. It meets coaches to Chester, Wrexham and Shrewsbury, every morning at 9, and every afternoon at 4, which are met at Shrewsbury by coaches from Bristol & c and all parts of south Wales. During the winter months, the Eastham packet. Joseph Parry, Master, sails every day, about two hours before high water and is regularly met by a coach from Chester.

Samuel Smith introduced further vessels on to the route, *Lord Stanley* in 1821 and *Maria* in 1824. The latter was replaced by the *Maria II* in 1826, which also sailed to Ellesmere Port. Smith died on 19 September 1827, but the ferry service continued in the hands of his wife Peggy and in 1829 there were four sailings daily to Liverpool. In 1834, the *Sir Thomas Stanley* was introduced to the route, followed by the *William Stanley* three years later. The vessels were named after the local squires who resided at Hooton Hall. William and Richard Smith were now running the ferry, but its popularity as a connecting route between Liverpool and Chester was hit by the opening of the Chester and Birkenhead Railway on 23 September 1840. Nevertheless William Smith reached agreement with the railway company on 13 December 1841 for his horse buses to use the station forecourts at Chester and Sutton. The charge for a one way journey on the buses was four shillings inside and 2s 6d outside.

In 1845, the Smiths sold the Eastham Ferry rights to innkeeper Henry Nicholls. He was keen to develop Eastham's potential as a day trip destination for people from Liverpool who visited the fifty acres of grounds of the newly rebuilt Eastham Ferry Hotel with its lake, ballroom, refreshment room, menagerie, bear pit, terraces and nearby woods to enjoy picnics.[16] The *William Stanley* was disposed off in 1845 and was replaced the following year by the *Royal Tar* (which was removed to the Rock Ferry service in 1850). The *Clarence* was added in 1847 and the *Loch Lomond* in 1854, but shifting sands meant the landing stage was difficult to use at times and rowing boats had to ferry passengers to and from the shore. A short wooden pier with fixed staircases was added in the 1860s.

In 1857, the ferry was registered in the name of Nicholls, Lawrence & Co, who purchased the *Thomas Royden* from the Egremont Steam Packet Company. The *Albert* (1858) and *Toward Castle* (1860) were also added to the fleet by William Hillian, and in 1861 HM Lawrence and Henry Gough built the *Eastham Ferry II* and *Swiftsure*. Gough became the sole owner of the ferry in 1862 and in the following year purchased the Loch Lomond steamer *Prince Albert*, which became the *Richmond*. In 1867, he acquired the steamers *Sylph II* and *Sprite* from the Mersey River Steamboat Service, whose service from New Ferry to Liverpool

South End had floundered, and leased the New Ferry Pier so that the Eastham ferries could call there. That same year saw Thomas W Thompson become a partner in the business and following Gough's death in 1871 he acquired the business and the five steamers *Swiftsure*, *Eastham Ferry (II)*, *Richmond*, *Sprite* and *Sylph (II)* and traded under the name of Thompson & Gough. In 1874, Thompson erected a short iron pier with a bridge to a floating landing stage (replacing a small wooden pier) costing £6,000 at Eastham and also developed the Eastham Hotel Pleasure and Zoological Gardens. Thompson also operated the Rock Ferry and New Ferry services for a time up to 1887 using the steamers *Wasp*, *Fairy Queen* and *Gipsy Queen* from Eastham.

Thompson ceased trading in 1893 and the Eastham ferry remained dormant until it was revived in 1897 by Thomas Montgomery of the Lion Brewery, Chester and William Thomson a Liverpool estate agent. On 24 July 1897, they registered the Eastham Ferry Pleasure Gardens and Hotel Company with a capital of £50,000 and in addition to reviving the ferry they intended to develop the hotel and its pleasure grounds.[17] In 1897, Montgomery and Thompson relocated the Jubilee Arch, modelled on the Arc de Triomphe and originally erected in London Road, Liverpool for Queen Victoria's visit to the city on her Diamond Jubilee, at the entrance to the pleasure grounds. They placed on the ferry station the steamers *Onyx*, *Pearl*, *Ruby* and *Sapphire*, joined by the *Eagle* in 1898–9, and commenced a service to Rock Ferry in 1901.

The hotel grounds brought many visitors to Eastham Ferry during the Edwardian period, most arriving by steamer as the nearest railway station was over two miles away. Entrance to the gardens was 2d and during 1908 it had 111,202 visitors when Fred Brook's Vaudeville Circus and pierrot shows were amongst the main attractions. In 1909, the grounds acquired an unusual attraction in the form of a topsy-turvy rollercoaster. This American invention, featuring a 360° loop, was one of the few rollercoasters of this type to be built in the United Kingdom and was originally placed at Crystal Palace in 1902. The ride was only at Eastham for a short while and was never particularly popular as a number of passengers received neck injuries after riding it. Outside the hotel grounds close to the pier was the Eastham Ferry Pier Bar, a beerhouse originally known as the Tap Vaults.

Nevertheless Montgomery and Thomson were losing money on their venture and on 14 January 1910 Sidney Dawson was appointed receiver for the Eastham Ferry Pleasure Gardens and Hotel Company. Between 14 January and 13 July 1910, Dawson noted that income received was £5164 with the principal revenue earners being the ferries £2219; Eastham Ferry Hotel and Bar £815; Tap Vaults £544; Jubilee Arch turnstile £386;

A view from Eastham Pier looking towards the Eastham Ferry Hotel c.1920. The short iron pier and floating landing stage was built in 1874 at a cost of £6,000. Marlinova Collection

The surviving stone abutment of Eastham Pier photographed in October 2008. The iron pier and landing stage were removed following the closure of the ferry from Eastham in 1929. Marlinova Collection

Gardens and Bar £289; rents £233; Vienna Café £245; school treats £149, Victoria Café £118 and entertainments £50. Expenditure however was £5669 and in the succeeding years up to 1913 only the period January to July 1911 showed a profit.[18] The principal loss earners were the hotel and gardens although between July 1912 and April 1913 the ferries were also in deficit for the first time. Dawson ceased acting as liquidator on 9 October 1913 and the Eastham Ferry Gardens and Hotel Company were dissolved on 25 May 1915. The business was taken over by the New Liverpool, Eastham Ferry and Hotel Company from 10 October 1913 but with the coming of the First World War steamer services ceased from Eastham. They were revived in 1919 using *Pearl*, *Ruby* and *Sapphire* but declined in popularity and were scrapped in 1929. The little pier lay dormant until 1934 when the bridge and landing stage were removed; the Jubilee Arch also went around the same time.

The stone shore end of the pier remains in situ, as does the sandstone booking office, the Eastham Ferry Hotel and the old Eastham Ferry Pier Bar, which is now known as the Ferry Inn. Visitors still come to Eastham Ferry to enjoy Eastham Country Park, which utilises the old pleasure grounds of the hotel. The park's visitor centre contains an interesting selection of photographs showing the pier and the attractions of the hotel grounds.

LIVERPOOL PIER HEAD (GEORGE'S LANDING STAGE)

Sailings from Liverpool across the River Mersey to the Wirral are mentioned in the Domesday Book of 1086 with a service to Seacombe. Ferries ran up onto the Strand before a wooden landing stage was built in the eighteenth century that could be used at low tide. This was demolished to make way for the construction of George's Dock and Basin in 1771, which gave sheltered accommodation for ferry boats. George's Ferry Basin, with berths along the Parade Slip was authorised by the seventh Liverpool Dock Act of 1811 although it appears not all the ferries berthed there as landing stairs at King's Dock and Graving Dock were used. Nevertheless problems remained at George's Dock with the ferries berthing at low tide and a run-out landing stage was built in the 1820s. This comprised a moveable walkway and landing stage hauled by chains up and down a sloping slip which was stored in a tunnel in the river wall when it was not in use. In addition a number of wooden landing stages were built for the ferries but they were often damaged in rough weather. The obvious need to improve landing facilities prompted Liverpool Corporation to engage William Cubitt to design a permanent landing facility. Cubitt built a floating wooden landing stage resting on thirty-nine wrought iron pontoons that rose

A postcard view along the 2,478ft landing stage at Liverpool in 1904 used by both liners and the Mersey ferries. Marlinova Collection

The Mersey ferry *Royal Iris* seen at Liverpool Pier Head in 1990 with the famous Liver Building in the background. Courtesy of Friends of the Ferries

and fell with the tide enabling boats to call at any time, connected to the shore by two wrought iron bridges. The total length of the structure was 508ft and it was 82ft wide. The new stage was officially opened on 1 June 1847 having cost the enormous sum of £50,000.

Although a great success Cubitt's stage soon became overloaded with the mixed passenger and goods traffic using it and in 1855 he was commissioned to design a second stage for the goods traffic to be placed to the north of George's Basin. The Prince's Landing Stage was built by Thomas Vernon & Sons of Birkenhead at a cost of £130,000 and was officially opened on 1 September 1857. The floating landing stage was 1,002ft long and 81ft 4in wide and was accessed by four wrought iron bridges. In the following year, the new stage was taken over by the newly-formed Mersey Dock and Harbour Board.

On 9 May 1872, the Dock Board authorised the joining of the George's and Prince's landing stages and the construction of a floating roadway. George's Landing Stage was also to be lengthened and an embayment provided for Lyster's chain steamers. The new George's stage, 600ft long, was floated into position on 24 July 1874 and was officially opened to the public three days later. Unfortunately it was destroyed by fire during the afternoon of 28 July 1874 started by a gas fitter carrying out repairs under the deck. The fire spawned a penny ballad that included the lines:

> The poor Cheshire people looked most awful black, they came o'er the ferries but couldn't get back, and one cranky Welshman got nearly smoke-dried, looking out for the steamer for the Birkenhead side.

Canada Works, the constructors of the stage, were engaged to rebuild it and exactly a year after the fire it was secured back into position, although repairs were not fully completed until April 1876.

The embayment for the chain ferries proved to be a navigational nightmare for those craft free of chains, and pressure was put on the Dock Board to fill it in. This was finally carried out when a new Prince's Landing Stage was built in 1895–6 by Pearson and Knowles of Warrington to cater for the transatlantic liners. When joined to the George's Landing Stage, the combined stage now measured 2,478ft, almost half-a-mile and had a total of nine passenger bridges. These soon became very congested however, and with financial assistance from Birkenhead and Wallasey, a new 25ft wide bridge was brought into service during the autumn of 1913. The southern end of the combined stage was further lengthened in 1922 by 55ft to enable the passenger berths to be moved south to accommodate a new landing stage for the Woodside goods ferries. The

Pier Head, as it became generally known, was now complete in the form for which it was to become known and loved for the next fifty years. In addition to the shelters for the waiting passengers, refreshment rooms, a booking office and a bookstall were provided.

The old combined stage lasted until 1973 when following agreement between the Mersey Dock and Harbour Company (formerly the Mersey Dock and Harbour Board) and the Merseyside Passenger transport Executive (who were to contribute 25% of the capital cost and a monthly sum for maintenance) work began on a new concrete landing stage at a cost of £1.7million. Whilst this was taking place, the ferry services were transferred to the liner stages at the Prince's Landing Stage. The new stage was to comprise six reinforced concrete pontoons, 197ft by 59ft wide, with the two southern pontoons reserved for the ferries. The pontoons were assembled in Dublin and were towed across the Irish Sea to Liverpool. A second road bridge was added to the new stage for vehicles using the Isle of Man ferries. The ferries resumed their services from George's Landing Stage on 13 July 1975.

The new landing stage however sustained serious storm damage in January 1976 that led to a temporary suspension of the ferry services. Two years later it became grounded due to insufficient dredging and on 2 March 2006 it was sunk when an air pocket in a girder was ruptured. A new landing stage was installed and was first used on the weekend of 8–9 September 2007 and a new terminal building has been designed for the Mersey Ferries.

Liverpool South End Landing Stage

This was situated at the foot of Park Street, Toxteth and except at low water spring tides, vessels of the Mersey River Boat Steam Company called there on their service between Princes Landing Stage and New Ferry Pier, which was inaugurated on 4 April 1865. The landing stage consisted principally of a floating pontoon connected to the shore by a 150ft wrought iron bridge built by Graysons of Liverpool.

Passengers using the South-End stage appeared to have been few in number and the number of boats calling there was reduced and then were ceased altogether soon after Henry Gough acquired New Ferry in 1867. The landing stage and bridge were removed following their acquisition by the Wallasey Local Board on 20 January 1876 for temporary use during the reconstruction of the landing stage at Seacombe. When this was completed in 1880, the old South-End stage and bridge were scrapped.

CHAPTER THREE
WIGAN PIER

The Pier that Isn't

The famous Wigan Pier 'joke' started in 1891 when a trainload of miners were held up at a signal box outside of the town. Across the flooded moss they could see the elevated railway that linked Meadow Pit with Newtown Pier and likened it with the pier at Southport that was well known to them. The joke was started at Lambe and Moore's gantry and was seized upon by George Formby senior (father of the famous singer and ukulele player) to become publicised far and wide.

Probably as a consequence of the miners' joke, a coal tippler stage on the Leeds-Liverpool Canal called Bankes Pier (after a local colliery owner) was renamed Wigan Pier. The tippler had been built in 1822 and although principally used to transport coal, it was also used for the occasional pleasure cruise. Before the coming of the railway, a passenger boat travelled daily between Wigan and Liverpool. The boat was pulled by horses and they did one return trip per day. When the passengers left

The pleasure cruiser SS *Thomas* at Wigan Pier in the 1920s probably bound for Liverpool. The coal tippler can just be seen above the right hand side of the boat.
Marlinova Collection

The 'Way We Were' exhibition building at Wigan Pier opened in March 1986 but closed in December 2007. Marlinova Collection

the boat at Wigan Pier they often called in at the Coffee House Tavern. The pleasure cruises continued until the 1920s, although in 1929 the coal tippler of Bankes Pier was demolished.

In time, 'Wigan Pier' also came to cover other coal tipplers. The 'pier' was further immortalised in George Orwell's 1937 book *The Road to Wigan Pier*, where Orwell dismissed it in a couple of sentences because he couldn't find it.

The pier joke was sustained through the years and in 1963 the town, in a bid to attract business, obtained the meter mark from the Royal Mail *Modern Wigan has no Peer*. In the 1980s the council decided to convert a neglected warehouse into the Wigan Pier Heritage Centre at a cost of £3.5m and this was officially opened by Her Majesty the Queen in March 1986. The centre consisted of 'The Way We Were in 1900' exhibition, a concert hall called 'The Mill at the Pier', pub, restaurant, offices and a restored Trencherfield Mill Engine. The coal tippler and stone base had been restored by a local college in 1984. The Way We Were exhibition, which chronicled what life was like in industrial towns and at the seaside, featured old pictures and postcards of Lancashire's seaside piers and the coal tippler. Souvenirs included a history of the pier and a stick of Wigan Pier rock!

However, on 20 December 2007 the Way We Were exhibition was closed as a new multi-million pound Wigan Pier Quarter development is planned to include an arts and heritage learning centre with the Trencherfield Mill Steam Engine as its centrepiece and retail outlets.

CHAPTER FOUR

SOUTHPORT PIER

Britain's Second Longest Pier which Nevertheless Only Just Reaches the Sea

Southport is a genteel, elegant resort best known for its attractive main shopping street, Lord Street, and the fact the sea is rarely seen in the town anymore.

However, once upon a time the sea came right up to where Lord Street is now. The area was covered in sand hills and was known as North Moels, the Scandinavian for sand hill. Churchtown was the principal settlement and its dwellers, along with those in the cottages on the shore at South Hawes, principally earned their living by fishing or gathering shrimps and other seafood.

The foundation of Southport itself is usually credited to William 'Duke' Sutton, a Churchtown innkeeper who acquired his nickname because he was fond of regaling what happened when the Duke of York passed through the area on his way to Scotland. In 1792, Sutton erected a driftwood bathing hut on the shore and six years later rebuilt his inn as a more substantial stone structure, which he called the Original Hotel. The name 'Southport' was allegedly coined there and a Dr Barton christened it in true naval fashion by breaking a bottle of champagne. Sutton's hotel was soon renamed the more suitable Southport Hotel, although it was known by one and all as 'Duke's Folly' because it landed Sutton in such debt it led to him being jailed and dying in poverty.

Cottages and marine villas grew up around the hotel and during the first quarter of the nineteenth century Southport's popularity for sea bathing led to its development as a resort. Longman's *Guide to All the Watering and Sea Bathing Places* c.1820 says:

South Port is daily rising in estimation as a sea-bathing place. It dates its origin within the last forty years and at present it forms a considerable village, comprising numerous neat cottages, most of them of recent erection; those elevated on an embankment called Wellington Terrace are very handsome. It is in contemplation to build a church, towards which a considerable sum has been subscribed. There are two hotels, and furnished cottages may be hired at the rate of from one guinea and a half to four guineas a week. There is a hot bath, as well as the other conveniences usually found at sea-watering places. The adjacent sands afford excellent facilities for equestrian exercises, whilst those who prefer water excursions may be furnished with safe and well-mannered boats. Other amusements are supplied by a billiards table, a reading room, libraries and repositories. Post chaises may always be obtained at the inns. Coaches go three times a week to Wigan and Manchester and twice to Bolton. From Liverpool the canal packet arrives daily at Scarisbrick, six miles from Southport, where carriages meet it from the hotels.

Boat trips ran across the Ribble estuary to Lytham and in 1835 work began on erecting a sea wall and promenade for which a 1d toll was extracted.[19] In 1839, the Southport New Baths Company erected the Victoria indoor baths and extended the promenade northwards from Nevill Street. The town's main shopping street Lord Street, named after the lords of the manor Peter Hesketh-Fleetwood and Henry Bold-Houghton, was laid. In 1842, the street acquired central gardens, which became a favourite rendezvous to listen to the band, and later blossomed into the elegant boulevard we know today. Coaches left every day from the Hesketh Arms, Union Hotel and Clare's Livery Stables for Scarisbrick Bridge to meet the boats from Manchester and Liverpool. The Eclipse coach left Liverpool every morning at eight and returned in the evening at seven. However the coach services began to fall out of favour after Southport was reached by the railway from Waterloo, Liverpool in 1848 and from Manchester seven years later. Southport ironically usurped Liverpool's position as a bathing resort. Liverpool had some good beaches on its north shore and a bath house was built in 1765 in what became Princes Dock. For a time it was the most popular spot on the Lancashire coast for sea bathing and had a full mile of bathing machines, however the bathing grounds were sacrificed for commerce and Liverpool as a bathing resort was no more.

In 1842, severe financial difficulties caused by his development of the town of Fleetwood forced Peter Hesketh-Fleetwood to sell his North Moels estate to his younger brother Reverend Charles Hesketh. He in turn soon sold the land in the town centre to Charles Scarisbrick, who had acquired the land of Henry Bold-Houghton. Scarisbrick was keen to develop Southport as a superior resort for the upper-middle classes and granted leases for suitable villas to be erected, regulated by covenants regarding value and building materials.

The earliest proposal for a pier in Southport was in 1844 in conjunction with a proposed railway from Manchester. An advertisement for the Southport Extension Railway, Pier and Promenade was published in the *Southport Visitor*, yet this plan for a commercial pier was not universally welcomed. Robinson in his *Descriptive History* (1848) commented:

An engraving from the *Illustrated London News* showing the official opening of Southport Pier on 2 August 1860. The banners across the front of the pier read 'Welcome Strangers' and 'Success to the Pier Company.' Marlinova Collection

In our times, a project has been advertised for erecting a railway pier to extend to low water, where vessels might discharge passengers or goods, to be from thence conveyed to the manufacturing districts. Whether this is practicable or not, we do not pretend to say, but it is scarcely desirable if a pier is erected as an additional promenade for the inhabitants and visitors, and for their convenience when embarking on pleasure voyages, it will be warmly welcomed, and will, without doubt, prove profitable to those who undertake its construction.

A further objector to the scheme was Lieutenant HG Kellock RN, the sub-agent for Lloyds at Southport, who proposed a ¾ mile long jetty on piles to be used purely as a promenade.

Eventually in 1850, a jetty was built opposite the Victoria Baths by local fishermen to take visitors to the pleasure boats. A ½d or 1d charge was levied to promenade on the jetty. In 1852 it was described as a *frail structure of wood, its shore end about opposite to the baths.*

In April 1852, a committee was formed by the Southport Commissioners (incorporated in 1846) to promote a proper pier for the town. Arguments raged as whether the pier should be used as a promenade and landing stage for steamers, or as an industrial railway pier for the transhipment of goods. The pleasure pier lobby was headed by Samuel Boothroyd and at a public meeting on 17 March 1859 it was decided to form the Southport Pier Company with a capital of £12,000 divided into 2,400 shares of £5 each.

The capital to build the pier was quickly raised and the design of James Brunlees accepted. The pier was to be long, 3,600ft, in order to reach the deep water channel. W&J Galloway of Manchester were appointed as contractors: their estimated cost to build the pier was £8,000 (the eventual cost was £8,700), and on 14 August 1859 a large crowd witnessed the first pile being driven in. The work continued steadily without too many problems and on 2 August 1860 the pier was officially opened with great rejoicing to the accompaniment of a grand gala, procession, banquet, illuminations, fireworks and a grand ball. Local traders were asked to close their shops for the day so employees could join the procession. The music was provided by the Band of the 3rd Royal Lancashire Militia and Fife and Drum Band of the 13th Lancashire Rifles. The steamer *Storm King* called at the pier from Liverpool.

Southport now possessed the second longest pier in the country (Southend Pier had been extended to 1¼ mile long in 1846) and because the pier was built principally as a promenade rather than as a landing stage it is sometimes referred to as the first true pleasure pier.

The completed pier was a marvel of Victorian engineering. The long and narrow iron structure terminated at a wide pier head measuring 100 feet by 32 feet, which contained seating for passengers awaiting the steamers. The height of the pier decking from the beach varied from 13 feet at the shore end to 22 feet at the pier head. John Dixon, later a notable name in pier design and engineering, was responsible for ensuring the solid foundation of the piling. Instead of using the normal 'driving' technique of inserting the piles, which were often fractured by the heavy impact of the monkey hammer dropped onto them, Dixon decided that Southport's sandy shore was receptive to the 'jetting' method introduced a few years previously by Brunlees. The piles used in this method were thinner than those driven and were open at the bottom end. A tube passing down the hollow pile was connected to a water supply and a vigorous jet of water aimed at the sand disturbed it enough to enable the pile to sink deep into the displaced sand by its own weight. Each pile usually took around half-an-hour to sink to a depth of 20 feet, and in six weeks all 237 piles had been fixed.

Whilst it appears that the provision of a pier for Southport was generally a great success, there were nevertheless some adverse comments. The main complaint was the long walk to reach the boats and the lack of shelter whilst waiting for their arrival. Others bemoaned the lack of refreshment facilities and the problems of ladies trying to get through the entrance turnstiles with their large dresses. The Southport Pier Company responded in 1862 by providing a waiting room for boat passengers and refreshment rooms. The following year saw a line of track laid upon the pier to carry luggage for steamer passengers with the trucks being manually pushed by porters. This facility, opened for use on 7 May 1863, nevertheless angered those who used the pier as a promenade: the position of the track in the centre of the pier was said to interfere with their progress along it. So far as the difficulty experienced by ladies at the turnstiles was concerned, the pier company could only suggest that they purchase season tickets which would enable them to use a gate to gain entrance to the pier, instead of having to use the turnstiles.

However, the pier company were moved to do something about the luggage track in the centre of the pier. In December 1863, it was decided to widen the pier and place a track of 3ft 6in gauge to one side where it could be enclosed by fencing. The line was also to be upgraded to a tramway which would carry passengers as well as luggage and goods. Work on the widening of the pier from three rows of piling to four, and extending it to the low water mark, was commenced in 1864. A steam-operated 4 HP winding engine was provided halfway along the pier and the 3ft 6½in wire haulage cable was attached to two 'knife-board' open cars that could each accommodate up to fifty passengers. The new cable operated tramway was opened in 1865 and immediately proved popular by taking passengers to the end of the pier in less than three minutes. However a fatal accident occurred on 1 August 1865 when a lady named Frances Bateman was thrown from one of the tramcars when it left the line and was propelled through the pier railings. The representatives of the deceased sued the Southport Pier Company and received £400 in compensation, while Mrs Bateman's brother-in-law, John Anderton, who was injured in the accident, received £250.

In 1867–8, the length of the pier was increased to 4,380ft when the 1864 extension, which had been built very narrow and several feet lower than the main structure, was upgraded and provided with a new 180 x 30ft pier head, which incorporated a plunge bath. The improvements were prompted by a proposal to build a second pier in Southport, to be called the Alexandra. However, this was rejected by the House of Commons in March 1867 on the condition that promised improvements by the Southport Pier Company were carried out. Another proposed pier, the Southport & Birkdale Crescent Pier, to be erected at the southern end of the promenade, also never came to fruition. To pay for the improvements, the Southport Pier Company regularly increased their share capital, which by 1874 had grown to £50,000.

To keep the pier select the tolls were kept deliberately high. To promenade upon the pier cost 6d and the occupant of a bath chair paid 1s. A single trip on the tramway was an additional 3d and the luggage conveyed cost extra. However, by the 1870s when Southport attracted increasing numbers of middle and working class visitors, the pier toll had to be reduced down to 2d.

The town's popularity steadily grew during the 1860s and 1870s with the addition of the select Birkdale Park and Hesketh Park estates. The promenade was extended by the corporation in 1872 and 1879 and in 1885 they acquired the foreshore from the local landowners and ten years later laid out the North and South Marine Lakes, joined by Marine Drive, and Kings Gardens. In 1874, the huge Winter Gardens were opened and featured a pavilion, winter garden, covered promenade, refreshment room and aquarium.[20] A number of large hotels were built to house the ever-increasing numbers of visitors: these included the Palace Hotel and Smedley Hydropathic Hotel at Birkdale and the Prince of Wales, Scarisbrick and Royal Clifton. The town's elegance led to it being termed 'the Montpelier of the North'.

Two further railways, from Preston in 1882 and from Liverpool via Ainsdale in 1884, opened up the town to more visitors and by the 1880s it was the third largest seaside resort in England. To the dismay of some of Southport's upper-class residents, trippers from Liverpool, Manchester and the other Lancashire towns descended on the town in numbers: on Good Friday 1876, 84 special train journeys brought 12,000 visitors, 8,000 of which paid 2d each to go on the pier. Over the Easter holiday in 1890 25,000 people came to Southport on Good Friday and 38,000 on Easter Monday, although over the next decade the town began losing custom to the fast-developing Blackpool. From 1895 a fairground was developed around the South Marine Lake with the placing of a bicycle railway and an aerial flight that carried people over the lake. Other rides were added in the early years of the twentieth century which included a water chute, Hiram Maxim Flying Machine, switchback railway, river caves, figure of eight railway and a helter skelter lighthouse.[21]

In December 1894 a section of Southport Pier collapsed after work on the construction of Marine Drive had led to water scouring a deep channel under the pier supports. The pier pavilion in the background was destroyed by fire on 18 December 1897. Marlinova Collection

Steamer traffic using the pier had also built to considerable proportions. Several small shipping concerns used the pier, including the Southport Steam Packet and Floating Bath Company and the larger Blackpool, Lytham & Southport Steam Packet Company who provided services from the pier to Blackpool, Lytham, Fleetwood, Preston and Llandudno. The *Lady* Moyra ran to Barrow and the Lake District. In 1880, the Southport Steamboat Company ran services to Lytham with *Water Lily*, fare 1s single, 1/6 return.

For a pier of such long length, it comes as no surprise that it has suffered a number of disasters in its time. Damage by storms was a regular occurrence and on 3 February 1889 the foundations of the refreshment rooms were wrecked during a severe gale. In December 1894, part of the pier collapsed after work on the new Marine Drive (opened in 1895) had led to water scouring a deep channel that ran under the pier supports. On 18 September 1897, the original pier pavilion was destroyed by fire, but it was replaced by a much grander building at the pier entrance designed by R Knill-Freeman and erected by WA Peters of Rochdale. Opened on New Years Day 1902, the new pavilion had an auditorium

A late Victorian photograph of Southport Pier; at 4,380ft the second longest pleasure pier in Britain. The buildings at the pier entrance were added in 1864 when the pier was widened and extended. Marlinova Collection

of 90ft x 53ft, a gallery on three sides and seating for 1,500. A year later, new buildings were erected at the pier entrance to replace the old 1864 buildings. The total cost of the entrance refurbishments and the new pavilion was £14,000.

In 1893, the Southport Pier Company became a limited company and took out a £10,000 mortgage to upgrade the tramway by replacing the track, providing new winding engines and engaging James Brunlees to renew the girders carrying the tramway track. A new safety measure was introduced when driver controlled grippers acting on the haulage cable were provided. A suggestion six years later that an additional track should be provided was not acted upon and in fact the track was shortened by 327 feet to 3,237 feet. However, Southport Corporation was engaged to convert the tramway into an electric railway using the outside third rail system at 500V DC. The corporation also renewed the rolling stock with a new motor saloon powered by two 25hp Westinghouse motors and two roofless trailers using existing bogie trucks of cars. The new line came into operation on 3 April 1905.

A postcard used in 1904 showing the new pier pavilion opened on New Years Day 1902. The pier toll houses were added a year later to replace the 1864 buildings. A crowd of people can be seen boarding the pier tramway, which would be replaced in 1905 by a new railway. Marlinova Collection

A feature of Southport Pier during the Edwardian period was the divers who entertained the crowds by diving off the end of the pier. This postcard features Professor Steve Osbourne who often dived off the roof of Thoms Tea House into the sea. Marlinova Collection

The pier railway features in this postcard view of Southport Pier by Valentines c.1907. The railway was opened in April 1905 to replace the tramway of 1864 and featured a motor saloon and two trailers powered by third rail electric traction. Marlinova Collection

A trip on the pier railway to the end of the pier would take you to Thoms Tea House and an array of divers who entertained the crowds. The two most popular and longest serving were Professors Osbourne and Powsey. Professor Osbourne, who began diving off the pier around 1903, normally dived off the roof of Thoms Tea House and performed three times daily at 12, 3.30 and 7.30. Professor Powsey often jumped off the pier on a bicycle. Bert Powsey was born in 1866 and performed until the age of seventy-three when he dived in aid of the Mayor's Forces Benevolent Fund into a water tank at Princes Park. He then became a lifeguard at the sea bathing lake before passing away aged eighty-nine in 1956. A further feature of the pier head was the headquarters of the Lancashire Yacht club.

A source of friction on the pier was the fact that fishermen landed their catches there and wheeled them along the pier in barrows, which often brought complaints from those using the pier as a promenade. The fishermen claimed that the Southport Pier Company was trying to drive them away from the pier by increasing the charge of their yearly contract in 1908 from 5s to 8s. However, this appears to be reasonably good value when you compare the cost with that of a daily promenade on the pier which was 6d. Admission to the jetty was a further 1d.

After principally staging orchestral and military band concerts, the pavilion was leased out from the 1906 season and variety entertainments were then provided. Charlie Chaplin and George Robey were amongst the variety artists who appeared in the pavilion. In addition to the pier pavilion, there were also outdoor entertainment stages at the pier entrance and on the pier head. At the end of the pier, Miss Blanche Laughton's Ladies Orchestra performed three times daily for fourteen consecutive seasons from 1917 to 1933. An evening's entertainment in the Pier Pavilion on Monday, 24 September 1917 featured the comedians Naughton & Gold, along with acrobat dancers, a violinist, female vocal duo, dancers and the news in moving pictures. After World War One the Pier Pavilion was renamed the Casino and dancing became its main attraction. The pier was fairly profitable during this period: in 1913 a net profit was realised of £9,155 and during the 1920s the annual profit varied between £4,500 and £9,000.

By the early 1920s very few steamers were able to call at the pier due to the silting up of the deep water channel. The SS *Bickerstaffe* made the very last journey to Blackpool in 1923 and by 1929 all sailings had ceased. The lifeboat station on the pier (which had been established upon its opening in 1860) was forced to close in 1925. By now, only the very end

A dramatic postcard showing the aftermath of the huge blaze which destroyed the pier head of Southport Pier on 3 July 1933. The damaged section was not rebuilt, thereby reducing the length of the pier to 3,633ft. Marlinova Collection

of the pier ever felt the sea, which enabled the council to reclaim a large area of the beach to build a municipal park containing ornamental lakes, a miniature railway and a car park.

The depression of the early 1930s led to very small profits for the Southport Pier Company of £1,610 in 1931 and £1,291 in 1933. Disaster struck the pier on the night of 3 July 1933 when the pier head was destroyed in a huge blaze thought to have been started by a discarded cigarette. The fire, which could be seen clearly from Blackpool, was tackled by three fire engines and 30 fire fighters using water pumped from the Marine Lake and from a hydrant in Princes Park. Miss Blanche Laughton's Ladies Orchestra, who were spending their nineteenth consecutive season on the pier, lost all their instruments and sheet music. The damaged section of pier was not rebuilt, thereby reducing the pier's length to 3,633ft, which meant that it slipped behind Herne Bay into third place of Britain's longest piers. In 1978, Southport was restored back into second place when Herne Bay Pier was wrecked in a storm.

Around £6,000 worth of damage was said to be caused, which the Southport Pier Company could ill-afford. In June 1936 the pier was sold to Southport Corporation for £34,744 and the Southport Pier Company went into voluntary liquidation and was wound-up on 31 August

The Pier, Southport   18745

Southport Pier's famous 'Silver Belle' train was introduced in 1954 and ran until 1972. Diesel powered, the train pulled four open and two closed cars. Marlinova Collection

The 'English Rose' train replaced the 'Silver Belle' in 1973 and can be seen here during the summer of 1982. The train ran until the mid-1990s when the future of the pier was very much in doubt. Marlinova Collection

1937. The new owners immediately put in hand the rebuilding of the pier railway's rolling stock, and further modifications were carried out in 1939. A green-and-cream livery, inspired no doubt by the smart Blackpool Corporation tramway, was adopted.

During the Second World War the pier was closed to the public and used to install searchlight batteries to probe for German aircraft on their way to bomb the docks of the River Mersey. At the end of the war the pier reopened and in 1950, on cessation of direct current electricity in the town, the Pier Committee of Southport Corporation decided to replace the DC electrically operated railway with a smaller railway of 60cm gauge. The new line opened for public use on 27 May 1950, but three years later the line's rolling stock was entirely replaced during the winter closure. The new 'Silver Belle' eight-car train commenced operations during the summer of 1954. This train consisted of a diesel-powered car at each end with four open and two closed cars marshalled intermediately. On 22 June 1959, the pier head suffered another serious fire.

By the 1970s, Southport Pier itself was facing difficulties due to falling customer revenue. Back in 1963 a new bar and café had been added at a

Following the restoration of Southport Pier, completed in 2002, a road train transported people along the pier until a new pier tramway was opened in August 2005. Marlinova Collection

cost of £28,000, however six years later the struggling Pier Pavilion was demolished to make way for the Fortes development of an amusement centre, bar and restaurants. Following sixteen years of heavy usage, the continued operation of the pier railway was put in doubt during 1970, and in the next two years the 'Silver Belle' was run as a smaller train until it was replaced by a Bo-Bo diesel hydraulic locomotive named 'English Rose'. For much of the 1970s and 1980s the pier remained very much 'as it was' and was a target for attack by local councillors for being a drain on the town's resources. During 1989 and 1990, the pier suffered storm damage and with it now losing around £100,000 a year and £1m needed for repairs, members of Sefton Council (who had acquired the pier in 1974 following local government reorganisation) called for the structure to be demolished. This resolution was voted on at a council meeting in December 1990 but was fortunately defeated by one vote. This near miss spurred the formation of the Southport 2000/Save the Pier group who aimed to raise funds and put pressure on the council to ensure the continued future of the pier. In July 1992 Southport 2000 and the Chief Executive of Sefton MBC agreed on the formation of a charitable trust to co-ordinate action to save the pier and prepare a £1.7m bid to

The new pier tram on Southport Pier which first ran on 2 August 2005. Seating 80, the tram was built by UK Loco at a cost of £325,000. Courtesy of Wilf Watters

the European Community to meet the cost of restoration and providing new attractions. However, disagreements between the two organisations led to a souring of relations and by 1994 meetings between them had ceased. Notwithstanding the internal divisions, the Southport Pier Trust remained in being and received a minor boost in 1995 when it was given a £641,000 European grant towards structural repairs. Later the same year the Trust applied for £2.8m from the Heritage Lottery Fund to enable the Grade II listed structure (since 1976) to be totally renovated, with the provision of a new road train, café, seating and wind turbines and solar panels for a new energy source.

The future augured well when the Lottery announced it was to pay for a £34,000 major structural survey of the pier. However, the results just confirmed the poor condition of the pier structure and it was recommended that it should close for safety reasons, which duly took place in 1997. In the following year the Lottery granted £1.7m towards the restoration of the pier and other monies were promised from Sefton MBC, the European Regional Development Fund, the Objective One Commission, the Ocean Plaza developers, English Partnerships and the Southport Pier Trust, who were also planning a sponsor a plank scheme. The rebuilt pier was to be 3,462ft long, built of steel and would feature a widened decking of hardwood, a new pavilion housing a café

The sea end of Southport Pier photographed in 2007 showing the pavilion opened in 2002. Courtesy of Wilf Watters

and observatory centre, and eventually a new pier tram. The work was commenced in 2000 and was completed two years later. On May Day 2002, the pier was reopened to the public and until the tram was ready a road train ferried people up and down the pier.

In 2003, Sefton MBC was awarded a Queen's Jubilee Green Apple Award for restoration work on the pier and the National Piers Society voted it its 'Pier of the Year'. On 19 July 2004, the Earl and Countess of Wessex, on a visit to open the new Marine Bridge, took the road train down the pier and inspected the pavilion.

The new pier tram finally came into operation on 22 August 2005. Seating eighty, the tram was provided by UK Loco at a cost of £325,000. The final cost of restoring the pier was £7.2m. In addition to housing a café, the pier pavilion also holds a collection of old penny and what-the-butler-saw machines.

Southport is now a thriving Merseyside commuter and residential town and remains a popular tourist destination with many attractions. Aside from the pier these include elegant shopping streets, fine parks and gardens, good sporting facilities (including six renowned golf courses), the annual flower show and the £35m Ocean Plaza complex with its Waterworld, multiplex cinema, leisure facilities, restaurants, hotel and car parking.

CHAPTER FIVE

LYTHAM PIER

Only Grass Grows where the Pier once Stood

Lytham is an old Fylde settlement that stands on the north bank of the Ribble estuary where it flows into Morecambe Bay. Mentioned in the Domesday Book, Lytham Priory was founded in 1190 but was closed during the dissolution of the monasteries by Henry VIII and in 1606 the manor was acquired by Cuthbert Clifton for £4,300. The ancestral home of the Clifton family, Lytham Hall was built on the site of the priory by John Carr in 1764.[22] The Cliftons became the most important landowners in the area with their purchases of the manor of Kirkham, and in 1824 the manors of Bispham-with-Norbreck and Layton-with-Warbreck (which included Blackpool).

Lytham became known as 'Leafy Lytham' because of the many trees planted in the area and it blossomed into a quiet seaside resort known for its elegant shopping arcades in Clifton Street, the Green on the sea front and the windmill on the Green.[23] By 1735, two bathing machines were available for hire, but it was not until the first half of the nineteenth century that the town began to seriously grow, with the Cliftons providing financial assistance for the erection of churches and a cottage hospital. However, tight building regulations were imposed to ensure selectivity, ensuring a proliferation of solid red-brick buildings to complement Lytham's *sylvan beauty and quiet tranquil air of development*. Hotels and inns such as the Clifton, Queens, Ship and Royal provided accommodation for visitors, who arrived by coach or the occasional steamers from Preston and Southport. In 1841, a dock was provided for anchorage by trading vessels whose cargo was then transferred to lighter vessels for the journey to Preston. Five years later a branch from Kirkham on the Preston to Wyre line was laid to Lytham following financial assistance from the Cliftons and in 1847 the Lytham Commissioners, who also oversaw the development of the town, were formed. In 1863, the Lytham Baths were opened and a railway built to Blackpool. The line was connected to the Kirkham branch in 1874, necessitating a new station for Lytham.

The provision of a pier for use as a promenade and landing stage was mooted for Lytham in the early 1860s, leading to the formation of the Lytham Pier Company in 1861 with a capital of £6,000, consisting of 1200 shares of £5 each. The Lytham Pier Bill gained royal assent on 29 July 1864 and work began that year to a design by Eugenius Birch for a plain pier 914ft long. Constructed by Robert Laidlaw the pier was formally opened by Lady Eleanor Clifton on 17 April 1865. The opening of the pier was reported in the *Illustrated London News* on 29 April 1865:

> Lytham, one of the three watering-places which are to Liverpool and Manchester what Margate and Brighton are to London, has followed the example of Southport and Blackpool in providing itself with a handsome and convenient pier, the shore on that coast being low and sandy, so that there is not convenient access to the sea at all tides. The new pier, which was opened on the 17th inst, was commenced in June last year. It was undertaken by a 'limited' company, and so great was the faith in its success, arising from the undoubted beauties and attractions of Lytham, with its park and promenade of a mixed rural and seacoast character, that the shares were taken up at once, without entailing any of the usual expenses attendant upon the promotion of such a scheme. The cost of the pier was estimated at between £5,000 and £6,000, and the actual cost has been about £5,600.

Admission to the pier was 2d although for those using bassinettes it was 4d and bath chairs 6d. Local boat masters could use the pier for

Four young ladies add charm to this postcard of Lytham Pier in 1903. The pier's imposing pavilion was considerably enlarged in 1895 and had its own orchestra.
Marlinova Collection

a payment of £1 a year. In December 1865 the Lytham Pier Company increased its share capital with the issue of a further 400 shares of £5 each.

A band enclosure was added at the pier head and in 1890 GH Bastow and the Famous Wood were engaged to perform on the pier. However, on 15 August of that year, one of the pier's supporting piles was broken when a barge drifted into it. The Lytham Pier Company carried out repairs and announced that a pavilion was to be provided on the pier about halfway along. Work began in 1891 and the building was officially opened on 27 June 1892 by John Talbot Clifton following a public procession. An orchestra was formed to play in it, which was led by Lionel Johns of the Halle orchestra. Touring and operatic companies were also a feature of the pavilion, as were sacred concerts on Sundays.

The cost of the pavilion however, which along with other improvements amounted to £12,000, led to the Lytham Pier Company being reformed in November 1895 as the Lytham Pier and Pavilion Company, led by a syndicate of businessmen from Accrington with a capital of £8,000 (8,000 shares of £1). Professor Hughes had been the diver engaged for the 1895 season and the steam yacht *La Gloria* ran trips around the estuary. Dancing and minstrels were other attractions.

On 6 October 1903 the shore end of Lytham Pier was destroyed by two sand barges, captured on this postcard by W Eastwood. Marlinova Collection

Following the October 1903 damage, Lytham Pier was rebuilt with two new shore end shelters. Note the advertising panels on the railings. Marlinova Collection

Lytham Pier in the early 1920s captured on a postcard by Valentines. The floral hall on the pier head replaced a bandstand in 1911. Marlinova Collection

George Kingston's Minstrels became an attraction on both the pier and beach by 1900 and there were occasional sailings by the *Ribble Queen* (when the notoriously fickle tides of the Ribble estuary allowed) to Southport and Llandudno. On 17 and 18 August 1903, the well-known comedian Arthur Roberts played in the pavilion and during September the Lytham Music Festival was centred on the pier.

However, the year 1903 was to prove a damaging one for the pier. During a great storm on 27 February two shelters were blown into the sea, and worse was to follow later in the year. On 6 October, an increasing wind led to two barges moored close to the pier, Nos. 5 and 7 of the Ribble Navigation Company, to drag their anchors around 6 p.m. There were two men aboard each vessel: John Quigley (master) and John McGuire on No. 5 and Albert Harrison (master) and V Menukenick aboard No. 7, who were unable to prevent their craft drifting towards the pier. Around 11p.m. the two barges crashed into the pier between the pier entrance and pavilion. Barge No. 7 went straight through the structure, bringing the decking crashing down, whilst No. 5 got entangled amongst the piles supporting the pavilion. Fortunately, further damage was prevented by a cable from the barge getting tangled up in a stump of a supporting pile. Picture postcards of the disaster were available to buy by the following morning.

A claim for damages was made against Preston Corporation, the owners of the barges and repairs were carried out in time for reopening at Easter 1904. To help pay for the damage the share capital of the Lytham Pier and Pavilion Company was increased by £6,000 in November 1903.

Kingston's Minstrels continued to be a feature of the pier until 1910. They performed daily at 3p.m. on the pier head and 7.45p.m. in the pavilion and there was no charge to see them other than the pier toll of 2d (1d for children). Divers were engaged each season to dive off the pier head at high tide and perform swimming displays: they included Professor Stearne (1907), Professor Alec Payne (1909) and Etta Mackay (1910). In 1909 a maple floor was laid in the pavilion for roller skating to take place during the winter. 'Rinking' (as it was known) was experiencing a boom at the time and there were three sessions of skating each day. Admission was 6d, with the hire of skates a further 6d.

At the end of the 1910 season, it was decided to replace the rather plain railings at the shore end of the pier (put in place following the 1903 destruction of that section) with new railings incorporating ornamental seating. The band enclosure on the pier head, which was very exposed in windy weather, was also to be replaced by Floral Hall seating 900 people. This was opened on 16 July 1911 and became home to Miss

A dramatic photograph showing the gaunt skeleton of Lytham Pier Pavilion after it was destroyed by fire on 29 January 1928. Marlinova Collection

Dorothea Vincent's Cremona Ladies Orchestra, who performed three times daily and twice on Sundays at no extra charge to the pier toll. Occasionally orchestral concerts were held in the Floral Hall at a charge of 6d (including pier toll) or 1s at the front. The Quakerites were engaged in the pavilion for the 1911 season and there were also visiting amateur operatic and dramatic societies. The pavilion also began to show films, which by the 1920s were its main fare. One of the kiosks at the pier entrance sold souvenirs while on the beach by the pier were Punch and Judy, swings, pierrot shows, donkeys, ice cream stands and sea food stalls.

In 1920, the pier company was reformed once again as the pier struggled to pay its way and in the following year the long time manager of the pier, JH Harrison, departed after thirty-two years service. Following a small fire a fireproof operating box for the cinema in the pavilion was installed, but sadly on Sunday 29 January 1928, the pavilion was totally destroyed in a three hour blaze. The fire was thought to have started in the gentlemen's cloakroom in the south-east corner of the building and fanned by a strong wind it soon took hold. All that remained of the pavilion was the metal skeletal frame and the fireproof operating box and these were soon demolished. The St Annes architect, Arnold

By the time of this postcard from the late 1940s, Lytham Pier had been closed to all but fishermen for the past ten years. The pier was never to reopen and was demolished in 1960. Marlinova Collection

England prepared a classical design for a new pavilion to be located at the shore end of the pier, built of Portland cement around a steel frame. Two new entrance buildings were to match the pavilion. However, the design was not taken up and no replacement building was erected. The pier was reopened on 24 May 1928 and still offered its Floral Hall with café and ladies orchestra under the direction of Annie Hunter, and later to Juan the Gypsy Violinist and His Orchestra.

Ambitious plans by the owners, Lytham Pier & Amusements Ltd, to convert the pier into the shape of a ship came to nothing and it was closed to all but anglers in 1938. By this time Lytham's sandy beach was being taken over by mud and spartina grass due to a new channel being dug in the River Ribble.

The entrance kiosks remained in use but the remainder of the pier deteriorated and the local children liked to chant *Lytham Pier is no good, chop it up for firewood*. In the late 1950s, the council took the decision that the pier should be demolished having refused to pay out the £5,000 need to save it. The owner Harry Kaniya received £4,000 in compensation and the demolition commenced on 4 March 1960. The cost of the work was £3,220.

CHAPTER SIX
ST ANNES-ON-SEA PIER

Once Elegance Personified but now Amusements Reign

Previously just a range of sand hills held together by starr grass, St Annes-on-Sea was a purpose-built resort that formed the western part of the ancient manor of Lytham. Eventually, in 1922, Lytham and St Annes were formally amalgamated to become the town of Lytham St Annes.

The foundation of St Annes was instigated by the St Annes Land & Building Company, formed in 1874. Prior to their formation, the Clifton Estate had laid Clifton Drive through the sand dunes to Blackpool and St Annes Road was constructed to run inland to join the Blackpool to Lytham road. They had also advertised building plots for sale. The name of the new resort was taken from the Chapel of Ease erected by Lady Eleanor Clifton in 1874.

St Annes Pier was originally constructed in 1885: a rather plain structure on deck level with just a small band enclosure on the pier head. Marlinova Collection

The Pier, St. Annes-on-Sea   *23rd april 1904*   Valentines Series.

Improvements to St Annes Pier commenced in 1898 with the addition of the two shop kiosks halfway along the pier. In the following year a half-timbered building designed by JD Harker incorporating a toll house and offices was added at the pier entrance. This postcard was sent on 23 April 1904. Marlinova Collection

The formation of the St Annes Land & Building Company was led by three men: Elijah Hargreaves, Thomas Fair (Agent to the Clifton Estate) and William J Porritt; the latter responsible for many of the properties erected in St Annes. Improvements to the railway in the area had prompted the trio to approach the Clifton Estate and request to lease 82 acres of land (later increased to 600) for a term of 1,100 years to build the new town. On 14 October 1874, the company was officially registered with a share capital of £50,000, consisting of 5,000 shares of £10 each. As part of the agreement with the Clifton Estate, a yearly amount of over £3,000 was to be paid to the estate and immediate works amounting to the sum of £70,000 were to be carried out. The original prospectus issued by the company proclaimed:

> … of late years, Blackpool has become so much the resort of excursionists that a decided want is felt for a watering place, which while possessing the same bracing atmosphere and commanding position on the coast as Blackpool, shall secure a more select, better class of visitors. The favourable circumstances under which the company commences operations, the whole of the land being

under one control and there being no fishermen's huts or unhealthy dwellings to remove, and no bad system of drainage to eradicate, will combine to make St Annes-on-the-Sea one of the healthiest, neatest and most cleanly watering places. The land possesses elements certain to ensure its development, the well-known salubrity of its climate, the nature and dryness of its subsoil, and the ready and direct access it commands by means of the new railway with the manufacturing districts of Lancashire and Yorkshire, will render it equally popular with many other of the seaside resorts for the which the west coast is so noted and thus justify the belief that the land will afford a fine opportunity for successful building operations.

The 600 acres leased to the company were divided up into building plots with leases of 999 years, with the last plot not being leased until 1963!

The original design of the new town was planned by the renowned architects and engineers Maxwell and Tuke to consist of elegant wide avenues and squares containing large and handsome villas and hotels of Accrington red brick. The first building planned was the St Annes Hotel, to be built by a subsidiary company the St Annes Hotel Company. The foundation stone of the hotel was laid by J Talbot Clifton, Squire of Lytham, on 31 March 1875 and it was opened in April the following year.[24] By the end of 1875, works to the promenade, public gardens, gasworks and railway (by offshoot companies of the parent land company) had all been completed and the first villas had been erected.

On 21 October 1876, William Porritt leased 28,940 square yards of land in Clifton Drive North and 42,000 square yards on North Promenade from the St Annes Land and Building Company. His distinctive properties were constructed of East Lancashire stone and the glass in the doors was etched with female figures representing trade, commerce and industry. Even the gardens were ornamented with patterns of pebbles taken from the beach.

A regulatory body for the new town, the St Annes Local Board, was formed in 1878, which became St Annes District Council in 1894. One of the council's first projects was the building of the South Promenade in 1896.

One of the undertakings of the St Annes Land & Building Company ws the construction of a promenade pier and in 1877 the subsidiary St Annes Pier and Improvement Company was formed. Work on a pier designed by A Dowson was commenced in 1879 but the economic slump of the period led to a delay in the pier's construction. The slump meant that some lessees failed to erect any properties and also led some of the smaller development companies at St Annes to go under, causing rental values of the properties to be halved. The St Annes-on-Sea Hotel

Company was wound up in 1879 whilst in dispute with Maxwell & Tuke over financial matters and the St Annes-on-Sea Garden Company and St Annes-on-Sea Public Accommodation Company had to be taken over by the land company.[25] The St Annes-on-Sea Gas Company also found itself in trouble and had to be supported with a loan on the security of a second mortgage.

Nevertheless, William Porritt ensured that the whole scheme stayed afloat (and virtually saved the St Annes Land and Building Company from financial ruin) by continuing to develop properties along North Promenade and Clifton Drive North until the good times returned later in the 1880s and saw the full-scale development of the resort return in earnest. Porritt's term as chairman of the company between 1881 and 1896 saw its fortunes revive considerably.

The pier was finally opened until 15 June 1885, having cost £18,000 to build. The official opening was carried out by Colonel Fred Stanley MP following a procession from the railway station to the pier which included Land Company and Local Board dignitaries, the Preston Militia, St Annes Band, St Annes Lifeboat, the Order of Mechanics and local schoolchildren. Following the opening ceremony and a ceremonial launch of the lifeboat, a grand luncheon was held in a specially erected marquee in St George's Gardens.

The main body of the pier was 912ft long and 21ft wide and it was an attractive structure, sporting the distinctive curved under-deck ironwork as previously used by Dowson on Redcar and Cleethorpes piers. Circular cast iron columns in alternate rows of two vertical and four raking columns supported four longitudinal wrought iron lattice girders and two bowed open-spandrel ones. The deck was composed of transverse timber joists and longitudinal boards. A small iron and glass band pavilion with seating was provided on the pier head.

At the end of the main 912ft structure, a 120ft iron extension to a wooden landing jetty was added in 1891, bringing the total length of the pier to 945ft. Erected by Messrs Garlick & Sykes of Preston, the jetty was 30ft high on three levels and was available at all states of the tide. The jetty was used by pleasure craft and fishing smacks, and also by steamers that ran to Fleetwood, Lytham, Southport, Blackpool and Morecambe.

The new resort suffered a maritime tragedy on 9 December 1886 when all thirteen of the crew of the St Annes Lifeboat *Laura Janet* were lost while trying to rescue the crew of the *Mexico* which had floundered in mountainous seas. All but two of the Southport Lifeboat *Eliza Fernley* was also lost. A monument to those who died was erected on the promenade at St Annes.

By 1900, the population of St Annes had reached 6,500 permanent residents. In addition the town boasted a number of large hotels, including the Grand (1898) and Southdown Hydro (1898), and convalescent homes, particularly for children. These included the Manchester Convalescent Home for children from Manchester Children's Hospital; Thursby Convalescent Home for miners' children from Burnley and the Ormerod Home run by the Church of England Sisterhood for Poor Children. The Holiday Camp for Manchester Slum Children was run by the Manchester and Salford Wood Street Mission to give children *a week or more of holiday and healthful enjoyment, and to teach them habits of industry, cleanliness and discipline.*

On the beach by the pier, attractions included twenty bathing machines with attendants, four sets of donkeys, two ice-cream carts and a hand-turned roundabout. From 1895 to 1903 Freddie Carlton's White Coons concert party were an attraction on the pier before they relocated to Carlton's Cosy Corner in 1904 (Gracie Fields performed at the Cosy Corner in 1913 aged fifteen). However, St Annes discouraged the visit of trippers from nearby Blackpool, the so-called ''Arry and Arriet' brigade, by charging higher prices and providing more refined entertainment. There were no public houses for them in the area anyway because the Cliftons thought they attracted the wrong type of clientele to the resort. The only bars were in the ten licensed hotels, which were outnumbered by nineteen churches!

Steamer trips from St Annes proved to be short-lived when the North Channel off the pier began to silt up after a new channel from Preston was cut by the Ribble Navigation Company. By the mid-1890s, the jetty was often left high and dry and the last steamer was said to have called in 1910. The loss of the channel also robbed St Annes the scour of the tide, and the level of the beach rose with sand (some 20ft between 1895 and 1925) burying all but the top of the jetty. The pier itself suffered misfortune on 15 August 1890 when the *Nightingale* crashed into it during a storm and broke two of the supporting piles. Repairs were carried out, but in 1894 the pier suffered further damage when a fishing smack ploughed through the structure during a storm, although once again the damage was quickly repaired.

The pier above deck level was originally rather plain and sported a dour entrance building and just a band kiosk, sweetshop and shelter on the pier head. However, in 1898 the St Annes-on-Sea Land & Building Company took the decision to carry out a vast improvement to the pier. Shop kiosks halfway along the pier were added that year and in 1899 a gabled entrance building in half-timbered style was added by JD Harker housing toll rooms and offices, and on the first floor the boardroom of the company.

The splendid Moorish Pavilion added to St Annes Pier in 1904, as photographed newly-built by Spring Bros in the town. Marlinova Collection

A landing jetty was added to the pier in 1891 but by the time this postcard was issued in 1905 it was usually left high and dry due to a silting up of the North Channel in the Ribble Estuary. Nevertheless the jetty still survives, separated from the rest of the pier. Marlinova Collection

A postcard of St Annes Pier in 1906 showing the improvements of 1898-1904 which included the entrance building, shelters, shop kiosks, the pavilion and a band enclosure. In 1910 the band enclosure was converted into a floral hall. Marlinova Collection

A feature of the Floral Hall for over fifty years from 1910 to 1966 was the St Annes Pier Orchestra, which was principally comprised of women. This postcard shows the orchestra in 1925 with their conductress Miss Clarice Dunnington. Marlinova Collection

The next stage of the pier's redevelopment was reported in the *St Annes-on-Sea Express* on 31 March 1904:

> It was in January 1901 the directors decided to widen and enlarge the pier, and Messrs Garlick & Sykes, civil engineers and architects of Blackpool and Preston were consulted and asked to prepare plans for the carrying out of the works. When the scheme was selected and approved plans were prepared to lay out before parliament to obtain a provisional order to enable them to carry out the work. These were deposited the following November, and the detail drawings were proceeded with at once. The Bill passed the committee and received the Royal Assent in August 1902. Tenders were then obtained from several contractors for the execution of the works and Messrs J. Butler & Co, the well-known engineers and iron founders of Stanningley, were the successful contractors; the woodwork being sublet to W.A. Peters & Sons of Rochdale and the plumbing work to A Higgingbotham & Sons of Idle.

The main deck of the pier was widened from 19ft to 34ft and continuous seating and open shelters were added. Lamp standards were fitted by Sugg & Company thirty yards apart. The pier head was improved with new refreshment rooms, an open air stage and a wonderful Moorish-styled pavilion, separated from the main pier deck by an ornamental railing with gates, turnstiles and pay box. The pavilion featured two ornamental domes at each end and a raised zinc roof in the centre surmounted by a lantern light. The building was painted a bluish-green with yellow tints. The interior was just as impressive: measuring 84ft x 56ft and seating 920 people, it was decorated in French Renaissance style with floral wall panels of light blue, light gold, white and gold leaf. The proscenium was decorated in gold and ornamented each side with large male and female figures. Above were two cupids and the letters S.A.L.B. (standing for St Annes Land and Building Company). Entertainments provided in the pavilion included orchestras, concert parties, operettas, theatrical productions and picture shows.

The open air stage featured pierrot performers such as Burton's Bohemians, Leslie's Comedy Cadets and Fred Taylor. However in 1910, the decision was taken to convert the stage and refreshment rooms into a floral hall. Designed by Arnold England, the hall was decorated with large flower baskets and could seat 850 patrons, who listened to the famous St Annes Pier Orchestra, comprised principally of ladies. *The Coastal Directory 1910* gave a description of the pier at the time:

> It has a light and graceful appearance, furnished with recesses and seats, and at the other end there is a covered shelter and bandstand. From the pier

head, there is a three-storeyed iron extension, which enables all passengers to embark at all states of the tide. It is acknowledged as one of the prettiest piers around the coast. During the summer a ladies' orchestra plays twice daily in the Floral Hall. The Moorish Pavilion has seating accommodation for 1,000 persons where performances are held by some of the best touring concert parties in the country.

The orchestra performed in the hall right up to the end of the 1966 season and it had five different conductors: Kate Ertl (1910–20), Clarice Dunnington (1921–33), William Rees (1934–42), Lionel Johns (1943–64) and Norman George (1964–6).

During the 1930s, Frank Monckton's Carnival Follies were a popular attraction on the pier and from 1940–52 Hay and Lancs Summer Revells hosted a summer show in the pavilion. In 1954 an amusement arcade costing £8,000 was opened at the shore end of the pier and was subsequently extended along the deck.

During the period 1947 to 1957 the pier made a profit every year except 1952 when a loss of £2,305 was incurred. The profits varied from just £186 in 1956 to £2,399 in 1957. The total income derived in 1957 was £13,395 which was derived from the following sources: Tolls £2,613; Floral Hall Seats £1,402; Amusement Arcade £4,208; Pier Rents £1,690; Refreshment Bar £1,929; Programmes £112; Lavatories £128; Deck Chairs £458; Motor Car Park £709 and Pavilion Entertainments £146.

On 11 March 1958, St Annes Pier Limited was formed as a wholly owned subsidiary of the St Annes-on-Sea Land and Building Company to run the pier. A loan of £3,000 was acquired by the parent company to help its subsidiary on its way and further income was derived from an increase in the pier toll from 3d to 6d (the first increase since 1923). On 11 June 1962, the pier and all the properties of the St Annes-on-Sea Land and Building Company passed to the London-based Amalgamated Investment Company Ltd for £240,000. The new owners added shops on the forecourt, an aviary and small reptile house in the children's area, and in 1967 converted the Floral Hall into a Tyrolean beer garden. An offer that year by Forte Holdings to buy the pier was rejected. In 1970 the Moorish Pavilion was converted into the Sultan's Palace, complete with belly-dancers, fire-eaters and snake charmers.

On 7 June 1974, the St Annes-on-Sea Land and Building Company celebrated its centenary with a concert on the pier by Yehudi Menuhin in front of Princess Anne. Sadly, just six weeks later, on 20 July, the splendid pier pavilion was destroyed during a night time blaze. In the following year the pier became one of twenty-seven listed for preservation by the Department of Environment, and acquired new owners when the

Sadly, both the Moorish Pavilion and Floral Hall on St Annes Pier were destroyed by fire, in 1974 and 1982 respectively. This photograph shows the Floral Hall alight in 1982, with the bare skeleton of iron on the other side of the pier head marking the site of the pavilion. Marlinova Collection

The entrance building to the St Annes Pier, dating from 1899, photographed in September 2001. Marlinova Collection

St Annes Pier photographed in June 2004. The isolated jetty can be seen beyond the lost section of the pier that once housed the Moorish Pavilion and Floral Hall. Marlinova Collection

collapse of the Amalgamated Investment Company saw the pier pass for £30,000 into the hands of the Webb family on 6 December 1976.

However, the pier suffered a further body blow on 23 July 1982 when the Floral Hall also perished in a fire. The blaze was said to have been caused by mischievous children, and bingo players had to be hurried off the pier. The owners of the pier, David and Michael Webb of the Dalmeny Hotel, engaged Fylde Demolition to demolish the wrecked ironwork of the pier head, which was achieved by gelignite. The length of the pier was reduced to 600ft, leaving the head of the jetty isolated.

Fortunately, the mock-Tudor entrance building survives and houses a café, shops and amusements. The amusement arcade now covers over half of the surviving deck and the open seaward section is currently not often available to the public.

Chapter Seven

The Three Piers of Blackpool

North Pier – Central Pier – Victoria/South Pier

North Pier
The elegant elder statesman of the Blackpool piers

The original hamlet of Blackpool was in the township of Layton-with-Warbrick and got its name from a peat-coloured stream that drained into the sea. The hamlet was first mentioned in the Bispham Church register for 1602 when the remote Fylde coast was dotted with just a few small villages. The commencement of the craze for sea bathing in the mid-eighteenth century brought a few visitors to the area to enjoy the fine sandy beach and in 1781 a road was laid to Blackpool on which coaches began to arrive from Manchester, Halifax and the other industrial towns of the north. When William Hutton visited the area in 1788 Blackpool had around fifty buildings, including inns such as Hulls and the Gynn

Blackpool North Pier photographed soon after it was opened on 21 May 1863. Aside from a confectionery and book stalls, the pier offered little more than a bracing promenade at this time. Marlinova Collection

This on-the-deck view of Blackpool North in the 1860s is of interest as it shows the outline of the tram track that was used in the pier's construction but was not put to use after opening. Marlinova Collection

to house the admittedly small scale of visitors that came at this time. Although they came on the premise of improving their health by breathing in the sea air ozone and bathing in and drinking the seawater, entertainments such as archery grounds and bowling greens also had to be provided to amuse them during their stay. Bailey's and Bonney's bath houses provided comfortable indoor bathing and the Baileys also ran a tavern, as did the Forshaws, another local landowner. By the 1790s, George Cooke had opened a combined billiard room, library, reading room and shop.

In addition to Bailey and Foreshaw, other local landowners included William Yates, who held land around the Lane Ends Inn, and Thomas Clifton, who despite the break up of his Layton Estate still held land on the sea front. To protect their business interests, none of them was initially particularly in a rush to develop their land, although that was not the case with Henry Banks after he had acquired the Lane End Estate for £6,000 in 1810. He laid Blackpool's first sewer to the superior holiday cottages he had built (available for £7 per week) and provided a rudimentary sea wall. Banks' son-in-law Dr John Cocker continued the impetus with the opening of the Victoria Terrace in 1837, which included a 100ft promenade, library, billiard room and seven shops.

On 15 July 1840, Blackpool was brought within reach of the railway when Sir Peter Fleetwood-Hesketh opened a line from Preston across Fylde to terminate at his new town of Fleetwood. Passengers for Blackpool alighted at Poulton station and took a 30 minute coach journey to the town. Two years later Thomas Clifton of Lytham acquired the manorial rights of Blackpool for £495 from Hesketh-Fleetwood and in 1843 purchased a large part of the old Forshaw estate. Clifton developed Talbot Road and Talbot Square and rebuilt the Forshaw Hotel in the 1840s as the Clifton Hotel. He then reached agreement with the Preston and Wyre Railway to open a branch to Blackpool to terminate opposite his Talbot Hotel. The railway was opened on 29 April 1846.

The opening of the railway allowed the excursionists to come in greater numbers and in 1849 it was jointly leased by the Lancashire and Yorkshire and London and North Western railways. Wealthy Lancashire businessmen began to settle in the town for the sake of their health and consequently helped fund the town's development. The Bickerstaffes, who brought the famous Tower to Blackpool, began their association with the town following the sale of Clifton land in the late 1840s. Robert Bickerstaffe opened the Wellington Hotel in 1851;[26] the same year that a Local Board of Health was established to govern Blackpool and oversee improvements in sanitation and street lighting and the provision of a gasworks. Funds were raised for the provision of a new promenade in 1856 and piped water came to the town in 1864. An early attraction for visitors was Uncle Tom's Cabin, opened by Tom Parkinson in the 1850s on the cliffs to the north of the town.[27]

The idea of providing a pier for Blackpool was first conceived at a meeting of leading townsfolk at the Clifton Hotel in December 1861. Two months later the Blackpool Pier Company was incorporated with a capital of £12,000 in 2,400 shares of £5 each under the chairmanship of Major F Preston. They announced that the pier was to be sited opposite the Clifton Hotel facing Talbot Square and Talbot Road that led to the railway station.

The chosen design for the pier was the one submitted by Eugenius Birch, who had built the iron jetty at Margate. An 80ft approach road lead to an abutment of 120ft x 45ft before the pier extended to a length of 1,070ft and a width of 28ft. The cast iron piles were to be placed at intervals of 60ft and the main girders of wrought iron were 73ft long. Altogether the pier would consist of 760 tons of iron – 420 tons of cast iron and 340 tons of wrought iron. Along the deck were placed ten kiosks.

Robert Laidlaw of Glasgow was the chosen contractor and they screwed in (with the assistance of Major Preston) the first pile on 27 June

1862. Laidlaw arranged for the iron to be delivered from their works in Glasgow to Blackpool by the Lancashire and Yorkshire Railway at half the nominal cost. However, the progress of the works was hampered by stormy weather, with the rough seas regularly washing over the so far completed deck. This led to the deck being raised 3ft during construction, putting an extra £2,000 onto the completed cost of the pier of £11,740.

The pier was opened in grand style on 21 May 1863 when a cannon blast signalled the commencement of the opening ceremony. The town was gaily decorated with flags and streamers and shops were closed as an estimated 20,000 visitors joined 3,500 residents to watch a possession of civic dignitaries and Blackpool Pier Company directors through the town before the pier was officially opened by Major Preston. The officials then retired to a dinner for 150 persons at the Clifton Hotel.

The original facilities on the pier were pretty basic, consisting of a bookstall and confectionery stall in the second set of kiosks, shelters in the seaward end kiosks and seating along the pier. Nevertheless the pier was immediately proved popular as a fashionable promenade: there were 275,000 admissions during the first year, followed by 400,000 in 1864 and 465,000 in 1865, allowing dividends of 12% and more to be paid. However to the dismay of some of the pier directors, who wanted to the keep the pier select, the 2d admission charge was proving too little to put off 'trippers' using it. Major Preston led a campaign to erect a second pier to cater for the trippers, which led to him and a number of other directors resigning from the Blackpool Pier Company and switching sides to the rival new pier. This was opened in 1868 as the South Jetty (later the Central Pier). HC McCrea was appointed the new chairman of the Blackpool Pier Company, a position he was to hold for twenty-eight years.

To counter its new rival, band concerts were introduced to the now-called North Pier in 1869, although the entertainment had to be in keeping in with the dignity of the pier, as recorded by the company's minute book on 5 July 1873:

> The alleged impropriety in the comic singing on the pier was considered by the Directors, and Mr Williams the Bandmaster was informed of the strict necessity that he avoid anything objectionable in the singing at the pier head.

In 1867, a steamer jetty had been added (which was widened in 1875–6) and in 1871 swimming and diving lessons were added to the attractions of the pier.

However, the opening of the Winter Gardens in 1876–8 heralded the arrival of a major competitor to threaten the pier's popularity. Further

Eugenius Birch's wonderful Indian Pavilion was added to Blackpool North Pier in 1877 at a cost of £40,000. Marlinova Collection

A photograph of a busy North Pier Jetty in 1882 with the *Great Britain* departing followed by *Roses*. Marlinova Collection

On 8 October 1892, the Norwegian barque *Sirene* was wrecked on the southern side of the North Pier entrance, causing damage to the decking and a number of supporting piles. Marlinova Collection

rivals included the Theatre Royal (1868), Raikes Hall Gardens (1872), Dr WH Cocker's Aquarium and Menagerie (1875), Borough Theatre (1877) and the Prince of Wales Arcade, Theatre and Baths (1875–81). In 1874, the Blackpool North Company announced that a £30,000 improvement scheme to the pier, which would include lengthening it to 1,410ft and widening the pier deck. Two large wings were to be added to the end of the pier to hold a sheltered bandstand and a 1,500 seat pavilion. Eugenius Birch was asked to design the pavilion; however, his original design was rejected as McCrea was keen on an Indian-styled building. Birch and McCrea visited the Indian Office to study drawings of buildings on the sub-continent and it was decided that the Temple of Binderabund would act as the template for the new pavilion. Particular attention was paid to the acoustics of the building, and at the back of the stage was an inscription in Arabic translated as: *the hearing falls in love before eye vision*. The Indian Pavilion was opened in 1877 having cost £40,000 and also added to the pier was a tea room adjoining the pavilion and new kiosks to replace the original square ones.

To help pay for the improvements the Blackpool Pier Bill of 1878 allowed the Blackpool Pier Company to be reconstituted and the pier tolls to be raised. By this time the capital of the company had been increased to £60,000. The rise in the entrance toll led to little custom being lost, as the pier prided itself on being a select resort for Blackpool's more affluent residents and visitors. In the Indian Pavilion, the North Pier Orchestra became noted for its high-class orchestral concerts under the conductorship of Edward de Jong and then Professor Simon Speelman. There were also famous visiting opera singers and instrumentalists, including Miss Margaret Cooper and Madame Adelina Patti, the Spanish Prima Donna and darling of Covent Garden, who's first of three appearances on the pier occurred in 1881. On Sundays after church, the pier was often packed with people promenading in all their finery. This was known as 'Church Parade' or 'Fine Weather Parade'.

Despite the 1880s witnessing a period of slow growth for both the pier and Blackpool as a whole, the town continued to advance in the hands of its enterprising first mayor WH Cocker.[28] Following the installation of electric lighting along the promenade in 1879, Britain's first electric tramway was opened along the sea front on 29 September 1885.

In 1892, the shore end of the pier was damaged on its southern side when it was hit by the storm-damaged vessel *Sirene*. The *Sirene* was a 150ft long square-rigged three mast Norwegian barque of 667 tons built in Genoa in 1867. She had a crew of eleven (ten men and a boy) under the command of Captain Anders Gjentson. In the early part of 1892, she left Christiania (now Oslo) for Fleetwood and discharged her cargo of timber without problems. On Saturday, 8 October 1892, the *Sirene* was set ready to leave Fleetwood to sail in ballast with just a cargo of cheap furs and jewellery for Georgia, USA, where she was to load a cargo of pitch pine. Unfortunately she hit a severe rainstorm in Morecambe Bay, and as the ever-increasing ferocity of the wind whipped the sea into frenzy she parted with her tug. The stricken vessel tried to make her way westward with shortened sails, but her forestays were parted and she was left running before a south-westerly gale in an attempt to seek shelter. As the gale force wind howled around them and strong sea currents swept them on a journey unknown, the masts crashed over the side of the ship, damaging the hull and disabling the rudder.

Finally, as dawn approached on the morning of the Sunday and the gale began to abate, the ship's ordeal enacted its final scene when she collided against the south side of the North Pier at 1300 hours, scattering the large crowd gathered on the pier and dragging away railings and decking. Four shops and a section of the promenade deck crashed down onto the beach below and several supporting columns and girders were badly displaced. Further damage was caused by the ship's bowsprit ramming the pier entrance. Fortunately the crew were rescued by being hauled on to the pier by the local lifeboat crew, with, in true tradition, Captain Gjentsen being the last to leave. The *Sirene* finally came to rest broadside on the hulkings of the sea wall adjoining the pier.

Once the tide receded, the ship's cat was rescued, seemingly none the worse for his ordeal. That was not sadly the case for the *Sirene*, which was declared a total wreck. However, Gjentsen refused all immediate offers for it and the vessel was looted for its cargo of cheap furs and jewellery, which (once the furore had died down) circulated around the streets of Blackpool!

Damage to the pier was estimated at £5,000, but it was quickly repaired. The *Sirene* was broken up where she lay, although until 1938 one of her spars held up a hoarding in Church Street.

Five years later, the pier's supports were damaged by the wreckage of Nelson's old flagship HMS *Foudroyant*, which had broken up during a storm on 16 June 1897. The wreck of the *Foudroyant* has gone down in Blackpool legend; no doubt helped by the ship's historic associations with Nelson and connection with the local football club, but also by the strange sequence of events following the disaster.

Nelson's former flagship HMS *Foudroyant* was wrecked at Blackpool during a storm on 16 June 1897 just to the north of the North Pier. Timbers from the ship caused some damage to the pier's support. The *Foudroyant* could not be saved and much of its timber and iron was sold off as souvenirs. Marlinova Collection

Named after a ship captured from the French in 1758 (meaning 'thunderous, flaming fire, striking'), HMS *Foudroyant* had been laid down at Plymouth in May 1789 and launched on 31 March 1798. The ship was a third-rate two-decked vessel of 2,055 tons with 80 guns on board. Sir Thomas Byard took command of the ship on 20 June 1798 and sailed her to Ireland in September that year. In June 1799 Nelson shifted his flag to the *Foudroyant* from HMS *Palermo*, where it stayed (under Captain Thomas Masterman Hardy of 'kiss me Hardy fame') until July 1800 when Sir Edward Berry took over command. The ship was present at the capture of the 80 gun *Guillaume Tell* in March 1800 and also the *Le Genereaux* off the Cape of Passaro in Italy. In March 1806, the *Foudroyant* took part in the capture of the *Belle Poule* and *Marengo*. Between 1807 and 1812, she served on the American station, and then became a guard ship at Devonport until 1892, when the Government sold her to a Mr Reed for £5,000. He in turn sold her on to a German ship breaker who planned to reduce the famous old vessel to firewood.

However, the newspapers got hold of the story and a public appeal was launched to purchase the ship (the asking price of which had gone up to £6,000!). Sir Arthur Conan Doyle was one of those who petitioned for the vessel to be saved and he even wrote a poem on the subject. A gentleman named Wheatley Cobb headed the subscription list with a donation of £2,000; and when public money was not forthcoming he and an unnamed partner paid the full amount. Furthermore, Cobb then spent an additional £20,000 in 1896 refitting the ship as a floating museum to tour seaside resorts in the hope of stimulating support for converting the *Foudroyant* for use as a training ship for young people. Queen Victoria paid a visit to the ship to give it her royal seal of approval.

Cobb sailed the vessel around the west coast, calling first at Southport, before it moved on to Blackpool and was anchored two miles off shore. This new and unusual attraction proved an immediate success and was visited by thousands of holidaymakers and local people, who helped boost Mr Cobb's training ship fund.

Then sadly it all went wrong. During the evening of 15 June 1897 a gale hit the town with full fury and the *Foudroyant* began to drag anchor. At 0900 hours the next day, the crew was forced to hoist a distress signal, but within a short time the vessel ran aground about 600 yards from the North Shore promenade, in line with the Hotel Metropole and just north of the North Pier. Throughout the morning the gale continued to batter the ship and by 11 o'clock her main and fore masts had crashed down into the sea and had been swept south with such force they caused considerable damage to the supports of the North Pier. All the while, the continuing ferocity of the sea had rendered the Blackpool lifeboat unable to assist until the turn of the tide at 1pm. Fortunately the lifeboat was then able to rescue Wheatley Cobb and the twenty-seven other men and boys on board (all dressed up as Jack Tars), but the *Foudroyant* on the other hand was declared a total wreck.

Cobb and his crew were taken to the Wellington Hotel to recuperate from their ordeal. On the next day Cobb wrote to his mother: *the huge old timbers are torn and ripped in every direction, every internal fitting and bulkhead swept away and the decks torn up and rent to pieces.*

However, Cobb appeared not to be too downhearted by the whole affair. He was wise enough to have had the *Foudroyant* insured and within a short time of the disaster bought the Bombay built ship HMS *Trincomalee*, which he immediately renamed the *Foudroyant*. That vessel still survives today under the care of the Foudroyant Trust in Gosport, and is the second oldest warship afloat in the world. In addition signwriters were engaged to paint in 6ft high letters on the side of the wrecked ship *England expects every man this day will do his duty and take Beechams Pills.* This blatant piece of advertising did not go down too well with the local magistrates, who ordered it to be removed.

Furthermore, wise old Wheatley, seeing the huge numbers of fascinated visitors and locals staring incredulously at the wreck, sold its timber and copper to the Manchester firm of Goodhall, Lamb and Heighway, who fashioned the timber into souvenirs such as doorstops, matchbox holders, walking sticks, newspaper racks and linen chests. The firm even published a catalogue showing the various items that could be obtained and in Blackpool a popular rhyme went *the glorious decks that Nelson strode, are now on sale in Talbot Road.* The copper was formed into 25,000 commemorative medals and medallions with a picture of Nelson on one side and the ship on the other, with the inscription *Foudroyant Lord Nelson's flagship commenced building May 1789, launched at Plymouth April* [sic] *1798, wrecked at Blackpool June 1897.* Due to the fact a large number were pressed, both the medals and medallions are quite easy to acquire today.

In addition, two more noticeable artefacts from the *Foudroyant* survive to this day. Hartlepool Maritime Museum has a large inscribed chair fashioned from its wood, while the boardroom of Blackpool Football Club is adorned with panelling that is said (but has not been proved) to have come from the *Foudroyant*. This had been fitted on the ship by Cobb during the refit in 1896 and was re-assembled in the boardroom in 1929. The wood was supposedly to have been donated to the club by a lifetime supporter named Eli Percival. In the 1890s he was a dealer in scrap and second-hand goods and so could have easily acquired the timber from the *Foudroyant*.

But that's not quite the end of the story. One of the local gypsies on the South Shore forecast bad luck for the town because Nelson's flagship was wrecked there, and to back her claim pointed to the very strange coincidence that the ship's conception, birth and death years all contained the same four numbers (1, 7, 8, 9). Her prophecies were dismissed as rubbish; but then for a time the town was indeed hit by a number of calamities, most of them connected with the *Foudroyant*.

To start with one of the policemen engaged in unloading the contents of the vessel was seriously injured in the head by a cannonball thrown over the side. Then, just a few weeks after the disaster, the top of Blackpool Tower caught fire due to an electrical fault, resulting in damage to the stalls and platform to the tune of £1,000. Fortunately no one was hurt on that occasion, but within a short time there were seven inexplicable sudden deaths within the Borough. Afterwards, on 29 July 1897, the salvage vessel *Anna* was wrecked while sailing to collect loose timbers from the *Foudroyant*, and unbelievingly her successor the *Aurora* shared the same fate on North Shore.

The old flagship, seemingly in conscious defiance because of its proud past, just refused to lie down quietly and on 17 August 1898 there occurred the final and sadly most tragic event connected with its marooned sojourn at Blackpool. By this time the Corporation had decreed the old ship must go, and while its final remains were being blasted into oblivion by Michael Hayhurst of Birkenhead flying timber struck Mrs Gates from Manchester while she was walking along the promenade and she was killed.

Now firmly established as part of Blackpool folklore, the memory of the *Foudroyant* continues to fascinate its people to this day and it is commemorated in a blue heritage plaque just north of the entrance to the North Pier.

Amongst the earliest of the steamers to use the pier was the *Belle*, which provided excursions to Southport in the 1870s. During the 1890s the *Clifton* ran to Southport, Morecambe, Barrow-in-Furness and North Wales. For the 1895 season, the newly-formed North Pier Steamship Company (Blackpool)[29] purchased a paddle steamer from the Clydebank yard of Messrs J&G Thomson and named her *Greyhound*. She was used to operate from the pier to Douglas (3/6 return fare) and Llandudno, and on Sundays to Liverpool.

In 1898, a scheme was put forward to the Board of Trade to extend the North Pier jetty. However, in 1905, the steamship company was taken over by the Blackpool Passenger Steamboat Company based at the Central Pier having overreached itself by buying the *Deerhound*. The *Greyhound* continued in operation for its new owners and during

A crowded North Pier during Sunday Parade in c.1910 when everyone paraded up and down the pier in their Sunday best. In the background can be seen Blackpool Tower and the Big Wheel. The latter was later demolished in 1928. Marlinova Collection

A Rotary Photo postcard of the North Pier posted in 1913. The entrance pavilion was added in 1903 and on the pier head can be seen the Indian Pavilion and the open air band enclosure. Marlinova Collection

The band arena on Blackpool North Pier c.1910 flanked on either side by refreshment stalls. (Marlinova Collection)

A postcard of the Blackpool North Pier Orchestra conducted by Professor Speelman c.1910. Marlinova Collection

The saddest day in the North Pier's history occurred on 11 September 1921 when the ornate Indian Pavilion was destroyed by fire. This postcard by the Blackpool Times shows the building firmly ablaze. Marlinova Collection

This postcard used in 1933 shows the pavilion erected to replace the Indian Pavilion destroyed by fire in 1921. Marlinova collection

the Following a period of closure during the winter of 1895–6 because the pier was considered unsafe, the structure was widened in 1896–7 from 28ft to 45ft and electric lighting was added. In 1903, the Arcade Pavilion was added at the pier entrance. Although the pier considered itself superior in tone to the Central Pier it still put on a wide range of amusements to suit all tastes. For those who liked their music high classical there was Professor Speelman and his North Pier Orchestra, while George Birmingham's Orchestra performed in the open air band enclosure on the pier head. Mr Birmingham was a proper dandy with his mane of silver hair, grey swallowtailed coat and a rose in his buttonhole. In the Arcade Pavilion at the pier entrance, Mr Jacobs and his Roumanian Orchestra played selections from musical comedies. The Royal Roumanian Sextette/Band was a feature of the pier from the Edwardian period right up to the beginning of World War Two under the leadership of Herr MG Fericescu and Herr Louis C Lewis. Ernest Lord's Excelsiors were a 'superior' concert party who performed on the pier. At the end of the pier, divers entertained the crowds with their spectacular leaps into the sea. They included Minnie Johnson (who also gave swimming demonstrations in a tank placed in the pavilion), Beatrice Kerr, Miss Scott, David Billington and Harry Crank.

The second pavilion on the North Pier met the same fate as its predecessor when it was burnt down on 19 June 1938. This postcard by Saidman shows the crowds on the beach watching the blaze. Marlinova Collection

Disaster struck the pier on 11 September 1921 when the beautiful Indian Pavilion was destroyed by fire. A new replacement pavilion was completed in 1924. Alterations were carried out to the pier head in 1932–3 that saw the open-air stand replaced by a sun lounge with a stage. For twenty-five years, from 1933 to 1958, this became home to the popular Toni and the North Pier Orchestra. A new bar and café were added in 1937, but a year later on 19 June 1938 the pavilion was destroyed by fire. This was replaced by a new 1,564 seat theatre with café opened in 1939.

In 1924, the prolific music publisher and songwriter, and co-founder of *Melody Maker* magazine, Lawrence Wright launched his *On with the Show* in the North Pier Pavilion. This popular variety show featured top musical bands, comedians, singers and variety acts, who performed Wright's latest songs written under the pen name of Horace Nicholls. The show ran until 1956 when Frankie Vaughan was the feature act: other favourites who appeared with it over the years included Frank Randle, Fred Walmsley, Tessie O'Shea (1934–6), Dave Morris (1940–6) and Albert Modley (1947–50). *On with the Show* was replaced by Bernard Delfont's *Showtime*, which began in 1957 and ran until 1982. This show also featured many household names: Morecambe & Wise, Paul Daniels, Freddie Starr, Russ Abbott, Bruce Forsyth and Des O'Connor to name a few. Charlie Parsons was a North Pier institution from 1957 to 1964. In the early 1980s the theatre was then leased to independent producers and from 1987 was split into a six week early show and then the main show, which has featured Joe Longthorne, Lily Savage, Brian Conley and Hale & Pace. On 1 June 1995, a fire at the back of the theatre caused £50,000 worth of damage. The blaze broke out at around 11pm following the end of the evening's show and leading the battle to fight it were the show's singer Vince Hill and Pier Manager Philip Lockwood. In the Sun Lounge, Raymond Wallbank commenced his twice daily organ concerts in the mid-1960s that ran until 1996.

The entrance to the pier was remodelled during the 1980s in a Victorian style and housed the Merrie England cabaret bar, amusement arcade and shops. The year 1991 saw two new additions to the pier. On 18 June, a £500,000 Venetian Carousel was opened: manufactured in Italy by Bertazzon, it took three months to build and could carry seventy passengers. A 250 metre long 3ft gauge pier tramway was added on 2 September built by Harry Steer Engineering of Breaston. The three single deck bogie cars were powered by a 2.3 litre Perkins diesel engine housed in the centre car. A heliport located on the jetty was also in operation, but this was curtailed when the jetty was extensively damaged by storm on Christmas Eve 1997 and was demolished.

A 250m 3ft gauge tramway was opened on the North Pier on 2 September 1991 and this photograph shows it in August 2002. However, by 2004 the tram had ceased to operate. Marlinova Collection

A photograph of Blackpool North Pier in August 2002 showing the theatre erected in 1939, the tramway, and on the left, the carousel opened in 1991. Marlinova Collection

In 1998, the pier, along with all the major assets of the Resorts Division of First Leisure was acquired by Leisure Parcs for £74million. They added a new heritage room featuring a photographic history of the pier in June 2002 which was housed in a new palm court alongside the theatre. The entrance foyer of the theatre itself was refurbished with a disabled lift and new seating and carpeting. The tramway received covered stops, yet by 2004 it had ceased running and during 2005 there was uproar over no live organist in the Sun Lounge. In September 2007 the pier hosted the World Fireworks Championship.

Grade II listed and now in the hands of Six Piers Limited, the North Pier is the most traditional of Blackpool's three piers and remains a splendid example of a Victorian seaside pier with a fine promenade deck and attractive kiosks. The pier received the accolade of Pier of the Year from the National Piers Society in 2004. The pier theatre and sun lounge continues to host live entertainment, whilst amusements are located in the shore end building. The carousel continues to function, and there is also a coffee lounge, bar, shops and a clairvoyant.

CENTRAL PIER
The People's Pier continues its tradition of fun
The immediate success of the North Pier led to a split in the Blackpool Pier Company. One faction, led by Manchester engineer and chairman of

The elegant outline of Blackpool Central Pier (then known as the South Jetty) at low tide c.1870: the under deck curved bracing on this pier was particularly attractive.
Marlinova Collection

A view along Blackpool Central Pier from the entrance in the 1870s. Advertisements adorn the kiosks and posters at the entrance advertise steamer trips to Douglas and Southport. Marlinova Collection

the company, Major Francis Preston, wanted to build a second pier to the south opposite the Wellington Hotel, whose owner Robert Bickerstaffe had promised to donate land for the entrance buildings free of charge. The opposing faction was content to build on the success of the North Pier and not to take chances with a second structure.

The dissident faction formed the South Blackpool Jetty Company in September 1864, and with six of the eleven directors also serving on the Blackpool Pier Company, an offer of amalgamation was made in the autumn of 1865. The Blackpool Pier Company met to consider the offer on 7 October 1865 with Major Preston in the peculiar situation of being chairman on the company who were considering an offer from his other company! The offer was rejected, and with the position clearly untenable, Major Preston resigned from the Blackpool Pier Company on 4 December 1865. He was succeeded by HC McCrea, who then held the post for twenty-eight years. Such was the lasting bitterness between the Blackpool Pier Company and Major Preston and the other renegade directors in 1866 their names were removed from the two iron tablets containing the list of the original 1863 company directors.

The Provisional Order to build what was originally termed the South Jetty was granted in 1866. The chosen design was submitted by JI Mawson for a pier of 1,118ft length and width of 24ft with cast iron columns, grouped 60ft apart, linked by wrought iron girders and attractive curved bracing. Robert Laidlaw, who had erected the North Pier, was also engaged to construct the new pier, and work began in July 1867. After a relatively straight forward construction, the pier was formally opened on 30 May 1868 having cost £10,000 to build.

The new pier was initially poorly patronised, being considered to be too far from the town centre and railway station. Fortune smiled however when Robert Bickerstaffe became involved with the pier; firstly as lessee of the refreshment room in 1869 and then as manager from 14 July 1870. He gave his first impressions of the pier:

I found I could do nothing on the pier, because nobody ever came on. The company advertised for a manager but nobody applied. I said if they could not get anybody else, well I would see what I could do. I took the manager's job on 14 July 1870. 'Try and see the summer out' said Major Preston, the Chairman.

Well I looked at the North Pier and it was crowded with folk, then I looked at the South Pier and counted thirteen people. I felt something must be done. We had a steamer, so I went to John Grime the printer and drew up a bill for the steamer to go to Southport that afternoon for a shilling, including all pier charges. 'You mean two shillings' said Grime, 'Don't make a fool of yourself'. 'Somebody has to make a fool of himself at this place, and it might as well be me', I said, 'When can you have them done, in an hour?'

I took all the bills around myself to hear what people had to say. They read the bill and said it was another steamboat hoax, for in those days they were in the habit of making people pay the pier charges themselves. I thought it was all up. However, to my great surprise, 250 people turned up at half past two to go to Southport. The steamer 'The Lady of the Lake' was pretty fast and I told the captain to keep good time and not charge the passengers anything.

During the afternoon I went out looking for a band of some sort. I met with one; I suppose it was German – I don't recollect. The boat came back on time and the band was playing; instead of going off the pier the passengers set to and had a dance, and most of them stayed on the pier all evening.

The popularity of the open air dancing was to be chiefly responsible for turning around the fortunes of the pier and the dancing would often commence at dawn and not finish until 10p.m. The dancing platform was originally located on the pier head before a central platform was added in the 1890s. Charging only a penny for admission, the 'People's

Pier' provided other attractions for its working-class custom base, in stark contrast to the superior clientele the North Pier catered for. The success of the pier was assisted by Blackpool's swing towards becoming principally a resort for the working-classes (although North Shore tried to remain select) who poured in from the industrial towns, especially during the Wakes Weeks. The apogee of Blackpool's success as a resort was reached in 1894 with the opening of the Tower. Initially promoted by the shadowy London-based Standard Contract & Debentures Company, the share issue was ignored locally until John Bickerstaffe acquired most of the shares and became chairman of the Blackpool Tower Company, enabling the Tower to be built on the site of Dr Cocker's Aquarium and Menagerie. The new attraction, which also included a lavish ballroom, circus, menagerie and aquarium, proved to be an immediate success and immediately put its rivals (particularly the Winter Gardens) in the shade. The Winter Gardens responded by opening in 1896 the Empress Ballroom and the ultimately unsuccessful Big Wheel (demolished in 1928). Bickerstaffe however was unable to save the doomed Raikes Hall Gardens despite his hand in the formation of a syndicate to run them: they were situated just too far away from the sea front. The grounds of Raikes Hall were given over to the boom in house building in Blackpool during the 1890s; a period in which further attractions such as the Grand Theatre (1894) and Empire Theatre (1895) were also added. The latter however was a failure and the opening in 1899 of the Alhambra complex next to the Tower (which apart from a tower virtually mirrored its neighbour in the attractions offered) was one Blackpool attraction too many. In 1902 the company running the Alhambra went into receivership and it was acquired by the Blackpool Tower Company the following year, which reopened it as the Palace in 1904.[30]

The Bickerstaffe family continued to be involved in the South Jetty and in 1894 John Bickerstaffe sold his paddle steamer *Bickerstaffe* to the newly-formed Blackpool Passenger Steamboat Company. The vessel had been built in 1879 by Laird Brothers at Birkenhead and survived in the company's service until 1928, when she was broken up at Garston, near Liverpool. The *Bickerstaffe* operated from a 400ft steamboat jetty which had been added in 1891. Two years later the pier was renamed Central Pier upon the opening of the Victoria Pier (later South Pier) at South Shore. There was fierce rivalry between the North and Central pier's steamboat companies, especially on the route to the Isle of Man. *Queen of the North*, *Bickerstaffe* and *Wellington* sailed from the Central Pier, whilst the North Pier had the *Clifton* and *Greyhound*. Sailings from the pier reached Douglas, Llandudno, Bangor, Menai Bridge, Liverpool and Morecambe. In 1904 the North Pier Steamship Company went into

The White Pavilion was added at the entrance to the Central Pier in 1903. Marlinova Collection

The most popular attraction on the 'People's Pier' (as the Central Pier was known) for many years was the open air dancing. The dancing originally took place on the pier head before it was moved to the centre of the pier during the 1890s. Marlinova Collection

"INVIGORATING, FASCINATING, OPEN-AIR ROLLER SKATING!"

| UNRIVALLED | HAPPY AL-FRESCO SKATERS, |
| "FIRMIT" SKATING SURFACE. | CENTRAL PIER BLACKPOOL. |

During the roller skating craze of 1909–10, an open air rink was added on the Central Pier. This postcard is advertising 'Invigorating, fascinating open-air roller skating' frequented by 'Happy al-fresco skaters'. Marlinova Collection

liquidation and it was acquired by the company operating from the Central Pier, the Blackpool Passenger Steamboat Company.

In 1903, the White Pavilion, designed by R Knill Freeman, was added at the entrance to the pier. An Electric Grotto Railway became a feature of the pier in 1908 and the Joy Wheel was another popular amusement ride. The craze for roller skating in 1909 led to a rink being laid and in 1911 the Joy Wheel amusement ride was added. Quadrille bands and, in 1912, Harry Jacob's Orchestra were further attractions. In 1913, the pier advertised its attractions as:

- Bioscope pictures every morning in the White Pavilion at 10.45 a.m.
- Fred Allendale's Central Pier Pierrots performing daily at 2.45 p.m. and 7.30 p.m.
- Open air dancing over the sea
- Military Bands
- Numerous side shows
- Swimming and diving exhibitions by the most noted swimmers of the day from the low water jetty
- Pier toll 2d, weekly tickets 1/6

In the 1930s, the 'Stratosphere Girl' attracted the crowds to the Central Pier by balancing herself on a flexible steel mast 98 feet in mid-air. A German girl, she was sadly killed performing the act in her homeland in 1940. Marlinova Collection

THE STRATOSPHERE GIRL
On a Flexible Steel Mast 98 Feet High in Mid-Air.
The Sensation of Sensations. The most thrilling
Outdoor Performance in all History.
Performing on the CENTRAL PIER, BLACKPOOL.
10—12 ;   2—4 ;   6—8 ;   Daily till 10th October.

In addition the pier was lit up with electric bulbs during Blackpool's illuminations celebrations, which were held in 1912–14.[31]

The years 1891 to 1917 proved to be profitable ones for the South Blackpool Jetty Company with usually a profit of between £4–6,000 gained each year. The profit gained in 1918 jumped to £6,713, gained principally from the following sources: daily tolls £4,679; four day passes £272; weekly passes £805; monthly passes £1 10s; annual passes £7; perambulators £23; bath chairs £1 11s; low water jetty £93; lavatories £44; shop rents £1,377, swimming £162, pierrots £4,158 and programmes £356.

During the 1920s, Wylie and Tate's Super Pierrots were a big favourite on the pier. The troupe's principal comedian was Little Jimmy Pullen, whose nervous bridegroom sketch and song 'T' trolley's off the wire' were great favourites. During the 1930s the pier offered the Stratosphere Girl. She was a German artiste named Erika who climbed a 200ft pole and swung by her feet to the gasps of the crowd. Her brother was often in attendance wearing a Hitler Youth uniform. Sadly Erika was killed performing the act in Berlin in 1940. This type of novelty act blended in well with the often bizarre attractions exhibited at the nearby Golden Mile during the 1930s. Luke Gannon was the major showman of the Golden Mile and his antics brought the crowds flocking in. They included persuading a local character named Bandy – so named because of his bow legs – to take part in a starving stunt, where he consumed just liquids for sixty days whilst lying in a glass case. Gannon charged 2d a time to view him. The starving craze caught on, although a Dutchman billed as the Great Sacko died whilst fasting in a shop in Church Street. Gannon then engaged newly-wed Joyce Heather, who had to survive ten days in a barrel without food and water. She looked set to win the £200 prize, but quit on day nine. The suffering of the poor girl angered people so much that they rolled the barrel across the promenade, bringing traffic to a standstill. Gannon's most famous client however was Harold Davidson, the disgraced rector of Stiffkey, who had been defrocked for befriending London prostitutes. Davidson was a household name and on his first visit to Blackpool nearly 10,000 people blocked the promenade to pay 2d a time to see him exhibited in a barrel (earning Gannon £850). Despite receiving a fine of £2 each for obstruction, Gannon and Davidson continued their antics and in 1935 the corporation had Davidson arrested for attempting suicide while he lay fasting in a glass-topped coffin. However, a doctor claimed he was in fine fettle, better than he was when he started the fast ten days previously, so leading to the case being dismissed! Davidson went onto Skegness, but was killed in 1937 from injuries received from a lion when he was addressing a crowd in its cage.

The golden age of steamer sailings from the Central Pier was over by the 1930s, although in 1933 Blackpool Pleasure Steamers Ltd purchased TSS *Minden* for local excursions. The vessel was built in 1903 and operated as the Mersey ferry *Bidston* and *Old Bidston*. She was broken up at Preston in 1938. In 1948, the low level section of the landing jetty was sold and removed.

The pier remained open during the Second World War and in 1945 Ray Barbour's Highlights began their association with the pier. So did Peter Webster, who produced the summer shows at both the Central and South piers from the end of the war right up to 1982. He helped put people like Ken Dodd, Mike Yarwood, Morecambe & Wise and The Bachelors on the road to stardom. The open-air dancing was less popular now and in 1949 the centre arena became an open-air theatre. Dancing still took place in an area on the pier head but in 1964 the pier's long tradition of open air dancing was finally brought to a close. In 1966,

The Dixieland Showbar at the entrance to the Central Pier 1980. This had been built on the site of the White Pavilion in 1968 and was rebuilt following a fire in 1973.
Marlinova Collection

Blackpool Central Pier in June 2004 with the big wheel added in 1990 prominent.
Marlinova Collection

White Pavilion was demolished and was replaced the following year by a new theatre seating 1,044 on the site of the open air dance floor. The Dixieland Showbar and Golden Goose amusement arcade were opened on the site of the old pavilion in 1968 at a cost of £150,000. Unfortunately they were both destroyed by fire on 21 September 1973, but were rebuilt and reopened the following year. The last remains of the steamer jetty were removed in 1975; the structure having been damaged in gales ten years earlier and the outer section removed in 1968.

A new entertainment centre named Maggie May's was added at the end of the pier in 1986, which is now called Legends. In 1990, a 108ft Ferris wheel was a very noticeable new attraction to the pier, which is now best known for its amusement and concession stalls.

Victoria/South Pier
Blackpool's baby pier now the haunt of daredevils
Blackpool's third pier was promoted by the Blackpool South Shore Pier & Pavilion Company, which was registered in November 1890 with a capital of £60,000. Initially there was considerable opposition to the pier from the residents of South Shore who feared it would lower the tone of the area. However, their fears were allayed when they were promised the pier would be select: there would be a 2d admission charge, no open air dancing (as on the Central Pier) and no shops at the entrance.

The pier's original design was submitted by the experienced Manchester architects of Mangnall and Littlewood. They envisaged a pier of 500ft in length and 190ft wide with a large pavilion seating 2,500. However, their plans were not proceeded with and the design of local man TP Worthington was eventually chosen. The pier was to be supported on cast iron piles and these were installed by the jetting method by sub-contractor Robert Finnegan in only twenty minutes apiece using a steam fire pump. The piles supported cast iron columns placed in double rows of six and the pier is thought to have been one of the first to use steel deck beams in its construction. Work began in late 1891 on the piling and by August 1892 403 piles had been laid. That same month, contractor Messrs Butler of the Stanningley Ironworks, Leeds commenced work on securing the girders and bracing to the piling. The woodwork was carried out by TH Smith of Blackpool.

The first section of 492ft was opened on Good Friday, 31 March 1893 and around 12,000 people visited it on that day, followed by 11,000 on Easter Saturday, 5,000 on Easter Sunday and 13,000 on Easter Monday. The Grand Pavilion, designed by JD Harker, was opened on 20 May 1893 with a concert by Edward de Jong and the 50-piece Pier Orchestra. The final finished length of the pier was 935ft.

Blackpool South Pier was known as the Victoria Pier from 1893 to 1930 and this postcard shows the pier in c.1910 in its original form. Marlinova Collection

The morning concert in the open air stage outside the attractive pavilion on the Victoria Pier in 1904. Marlinova Collection

A postcard from 1904 showing the interior of the Blackpool Victoria Pier Pavilion, which was designed by JD Harker. Marlinova Collection

The Victoria Pier featured on a postcard from the 1920s showing the Regal Theatre at the entrance, home to Ernest Binns' Arcadian Follies, a feature of the pier throughout the 1920s and 1930s. Marlinova Collection

Aside from the Grand Pavilion, the pier's initial attractions included a bandstand, thirty-six shops, shelters and open air stage at the end of the pier. Admission was 2d and the pier prided itself on the fact it offered refined entertainment as 'Blackpool's Elite Rendezvous'. In addition to the Pier Orchestra (led by JW Collinson), other regular attractions on the pier included Herr Arnold Blome and His Viennese Orchestra (who performed in the bandstand when fine and the pavilion when wet), Flockton Foster's troupe (in the open air stage) and Miss Vera Bosisto's Ladies Orchestra. Military and brass bands also featured. Sam Hague's Minstrels performed on the pier in 1899 and Adeler and Sutton's Pierrots, featuring Charlie Harvey, were a feature from 1903 to 1908. George Royle's Troubadors were engaged before they moved to Scarborough to become the Imps and then the celebrated Fol-de-Rols. Fred Walmsley's Tonics were based on the pier between 1909 and 1925 before Walmsley moved to the North Pier to become the comedy star of Lawrence Wright's annual *On with the Show*. The Victoria Pavilion was added to the front of the pier in 1911 to house the pierrot and concert party shows and had a capacity to hold 900 people.

Although situated some distance from the other two piers and the Tower, the success of the Victoria Pier was assisted somewhat by the popularity of the nearby Pleasure Beach amusement park, which is currently Europe's largest amusement park and one of its most visited

The 1936 line-up of Ernest Binns' popular Arcadian Follies on Blackpool South Pier. Mr Binns is the man in the centre of the picture. Marlinova Collection

attractions. The origins of the Pleasure Beach dated back to 1891 when a switchback railway was placed among the sand dunes amidst a gypsy encampment. In 1895, John Outhwaite opened a roundabout near the switchback, and in the following year he went into partnership with William Bean who erected a Hotchkiss Bicycle Railway that he had brought back from America. The success of the park began to really take off following the placement of the Hiram Maxim Flying Machine (1904), River Caves (1905), LA Thompson Scenic Railway (1907) and Velvet Coaster (1909) and by 1909 the park was the biggest and most modern in the country.

During the 1920s Blackpool Corporation added an open air swimming pool to South Shore and extended the promenade to Squires Gate. In responding to popular tastes, the Victoria Pier added a floral hall at the end of the pier (on the site of the open-air stage) and cinema. Seats in the Floral Hall were free except on Sundays and for special events when they were 4d and 7d. Between 1919 and 1926 Jan Hurst was conductor of the Regal Court Orchestra and after spells at Bridlington, Bath, Brighton and Lowestoft returned to the pier for a second spell in 1936–9.

In 1930, the pier was renamed the South Pier at the suggestion of Harry Korris who ran the popular Arcadian Follies with Ernest Binns on the pier from 1931 to 1939. They principally performed in the Regal Theatre, built in 1938 of reinforced concrete on the site of the Victoria Pavilion. The pier had to be widened by 20ft and the substructure of the new theatre built of concrete on piles driven to a depth of 40ft below beach level. Designed by RW Hurst and DR Humphreys of London, the theatre could seat 1,300 patrons and was officially opened on 27 June 1938.

The period between the wars saw the pier just about pay its way, although such dividends paid to shareholders were small and often none were paid at all. The best dividend proved to be after the war in 1948 when 15% was paid.

During the Second World War the pier remained open and Jack 'Tinker' Taylor's variety shows were a feature in the Regal Theatre during the 1940s. After the war the Rainbow Pierrots/Revels kept up the pierrot tradition on the pier in the Rainbow Theatre (formerly the Grand Theatre) and featured Charlie Parsons in 1952–6. Peter Webster produced shows on the pier before moving to the Central Pier, where he nurtured many a talent to fame. Dave Morris' club nights brought the crowds onto the pier in the 1950s and 1960s and many well-known comedians, musical acts and comedians appeared there. Unfortunately, the Grand Pavilion, then known as the Rainbow Theatre, was damaged by fire in 1954 and 1958 before being destroyed altogether during the

The Regal Theatre at the South Pier photographed in the late 1940s. The building was converted into an amusement arcade in 1966. Marlinova Collection

The 'Adrenaline Zone' at the end of Blackpool South Pier in June 2004 featuring the Reverse Bungy and SCAD diving attraction. Marlinova Collection

evening of 6 February 1964: a replacement was quickly built however at a cost of £90,000. Two years earlier, the Regal Theatre at the pier entrance had been converted into the Beachcomber amusement arcade.

In 1968, the pier was acquired by Trust House Forte, who held it until 1983 when First Leisure took over. They replaced the decking of the pier in 1985 with 40,000ft of African opepe wood, which is so hard that it is impossible to hammer nails into it, and restyled the frontage of the pier with a circus look.

Subsequently in the hands of Leisure Parcs and now Six Piers Limited, the emphasis in recent years has been to convert the pier head into an amusement park. In 1998, the theatre was removed to make way for a new £1.5m white knuckle ride called the Spinning Mouse. Two years later the country's fastest amusement ride, the Reverse Bungy, was added to the pier. The ride catapulted its customers 180ft into the air at a speed of 2,000km/ph. In 2001, the pier acquired the SCAD diving attraction, fully justifying the amusement area's tag as the Adrenaline Zone.

CHAPTER EIGHT

FLEETWOOD PIER

A Cinderella Pier left to Linger and Die

Fleetwood was the creation of Sir Peter Hesketh-Fleetwood[32] who had inherited the family estates in 1824, which included land at North Meols (present-day Southport), Blackpool and the Manor of Rossall at the tip of the Fylde Peninsular around the River Wyre. In 1830, in his position as High Sheriff of Lancashire, he attended the opening of the Liverpool and Manchester Railway and this gave him the idea of developing his Rossall Estate as a port and watering place and connecting it by rail to Preston.[33] At the time the area was rather desolate and was home to grass-covered dunes, sea birds and rabbits. The name 'Fleetwood' was chosen for the new town by deed poll in 1831 and three years later Hesketh-Fleetwood published the *Preston and Wyre Prospectus and Plans* with the support of a number of local landowners and businessmen. The building of the Fleetwood commenced with the erection of the Fleetwood Arms Hotel in 1836 and Hesketh engaged the noted architect Decimus Burton to design a plan for the town. He used the Mount, the most northerly of the Starr hills on the Fylde coast, as the centre point and arranged for the streets to radiate from it like the spokes of a wheel.

The single track railway arrived from Preston on 15 July 1840 and for a time Fleetwood was the terminus of the London and North Western Railway line from Euston and provided connecting boat services from its new dock to Belfast, Ardrossan and the Isle of Man.[34] The port also became the principal fishing port on the west coast as its entrance channel was easy to navigate. By 1841, the population had reached 2,833 and Burton was starting work on Queens Terrace, a superior row of eight town houses close to the river estuary that was completed in 1844. The impressive North Euston Hotel was opened to visitors staying in the town in 1841 although it was never fully completed to its original design. Three lighthouses were provided at different levels on the same line to navigate vessels into the port. The tallest lighthouse, standing 90ft above high water mark, was erected in Pharos Place whilst the lower light was provided on the Esplanade: both were designed by Decimus Burton and built by John Tomkinson. The third light was at the entrance to the channel and was built on top of seven iron screw piles designed by Alexander Mitchell.

The cost of building the new town and railway however brought Peter Hesketh-Fleetwood to his knees. George Landmann's estimate for building the railway for example was far lower than what it actually cost and Hesketh's agent Frederick Kent failed to collect the rents that were due to him. The ancestral home at Rossall Hall was leased and all of its contents were sold off. In 1842 the town was placed in to the hands of the Fleetwood Improvement Commissioners.

The select intentions of the new resort initially attracted the nobility although day trippers also came on the new railway on special half price days. Early entertainments included climbing the 94 steps of the Pharos Lighthouse, boat trips, donkey and pony rides on the beach and dancing on the Mount. As a resort however Fleetwood was soon overtaken by nearby Blackpool, although its quiet resort area did have its followers. As Blackpool threw itself wholeheartedly into being a major seaside resort, Fleetwood couldn't quite make its mind up whether it was a commercial port, fishing port, seaside resort or all three. In 1859, a ferry service was commenced across to the small seaside village of Knott End and in 1898 the Blackpool and Fleetwood Tramroad arrived in the town.

The first proposal for a pier for Fleetwood was made by the town commissioner Richard Edmundson in 1892 but the plan was met with opposition from the Lancashire and Yorkshire Railway Company and

A postcard of Fleetwood Pier soon after it was opened in 1910 to a length of 492ft. The pavilion was added in 1911. Marlinova Collection

there were concerns that the pier would be hazardous to shipping in the area. A scheme to build a pier at the end of Bold Street also failed when a printer named Thomas Woods objected. A further attempt by the Fleetwood Pier Company to provide the town with a 1,290ft pier in 1899 was approved by Fleetwood UDC but once again concerns were raised that a pier of such length would be a danger to shipping. Finally, a revised prospectus and plan submitted by the Fleetwood Pier Company were approved in 1906 for a 700ft pier extending from Fielden Esplanade. In the following year the Fleetwood Pier Company was reformed as the Fleetwood Victoria Pier Company, led by Olympia (IOM) Ltd, based in Douglas, Isle of Man. The Fleetwood Victoria Pier Order was gained that year and the company was floated with a capital of £30,000 in £1 shares. The pier design of Blackpool architect Tom Lumb was chosen: Lumb had previously been involved with the construction of the Blackpool and Fleetwood Tramroad. The contractors Gradwell of Barrow commenced building the pier in 1909 and it was completed the following year to a length of 492ft: a lack of capital necessitating a shorter pier than originally envisaged. The pier was the last to be built during the Golden Age of pier construction between 1855 and 1910. On 19 June 1911 the pier acquired a pavilion at the entrance.

By the 1940s, the frontage of Fleetwood Pier had been remodelled with cafes and amusements and was one of the very few piers with free admission. Marlinova Collection

On 20 August 1952, the pavilion of Fleetwood Pier was destroyed in one of the biggest fires the town had witnessed. Marlinova Collection

Fleetwood Pier in the 1960s, with a remodelled frontage that incorporated a large bingo hall, café, Jolly Roger bar and amusements. Marlinova Collection

In October 1919, the Fleetwood Victoria Pier Company sold the pier to the Fleetwood Pier and Pavilion Company, although Olympia (IOM) retained an interest. The new company had been formed by fish salesman Rowland Morris and steam trawler owner Joseph Taylor with a capital of £20,000 in £1 shares. In 1936 the company was revamped again when its directors put it into voluntary liquidation and formed the Fleetwood Pier Company with a capital of £60,000 which consisted of 120,000 Cumulative Preference Shares of 5s and 600,000 ordinary 1s shares.

On 20 August 1952, the pier pavilion was destroyed in the biggest fire Fleetwood has ever seen. The blaze, which could be seen twenty miles away, was watched by huge crowd from 10.30 p.m. to midnight and was thought to have begun behind a cinema screen. Eight fire engines attended the fire and Councillor EF Mickie organised a human chain to rescue anything off the pier they could. The pier was reduced to a tangled mass of charred steel and the damage was estimated at £40,000. On the following morning, scores of fortune seekers searched underneath the pier for coins from the machines, but many had been fused together by the intense heat.

The pier was not fully restored until 1958 and seven years later changed hands when it was acquired by the Manzi Brothers for £80,000 (£50,000 for the pier and £30,000 for the fixtures and fittings). The Manzis owned two large amusement arcades in Southend-on-Sea and were partners in a large amusement arcade in Blackpool. A large bingo hall and amusements were added to the pier and a further feature was Jollies Bar and a cafeteria seating 250. The pier advertised itself as one of the few piers free to enter. In 1972, the pier received another facelift at a cost of £70.000. During the summers of 1975 and 1976 the Fleetwood Pier Company operated the 'Santa Fe' miniature railway along the sea front from the pier to Beach Road. The engine was sold however to a firm in Aberdeen and the track now llies buried under the sand.

In 2000, the pier was closed after the owners Fleetwood Amusements Ltd went into liquidation. Two years later Cheshire businessman Doug Glendon acquired the pier on a seventy year lease and announced a £2.2 million project in association with brewers Carlsberg-Tetley to create a major live entertainment complex, revamp Jollies Bar, reopen the bingo operation and update the amusement arcade. Nothing came of this plan and in 2005 the pier was sold by the Iranian businessman Mehdi Ashfar to a Manchester-based investment and property company. They put the pier up for sale in June 2006 but refused an offer of £1.28 million. They tried again on 21 February 2007 when the pier was offered for sale by auction at Manchester Airport. However, the highest bid was just £490,000 and

Fleetwood Pier photographed on a rainy day in September 2001, by which time only the amusement arcade was open and the pier was in a run-down condition.
Marlinova Collection

Following its acquisition by Doug Glendon in 2002, the frontage of Fleetwood Pier was restyled. However ambitious, plans to revamp the whole pier came to nothing.
Marlinova Collection

During the early hours of 9 September 2008 the buildings on Fleetwood Pier were destroyed by fire and what remained was pulled down the following month. So ended the life of Fleetwood Pier, two years short of its centenary. Marlinova Collection

the reserve was not reached. Two months later the pier was acquired by local entertainer Mike Simmons, known professionally as Joey Blower. He published plans to erect luxury flats across the entrance to the pier and retain the structure perhaps to be used as a private promenade for the residents. However, in the early hours of Tuesday 9 September 2008 the pier buildings were destroyed in a fire. Fire crews were called to the pier at 4.30am after smoke was seen rising from the main building at the front of the pier. More than seventy fire fighters fought the blaze which completely gutted the building. The shattered remains of the pier were demolished the following month, and Fleetwood Pier passed into history.

CHAPTER NINE

MORECAMBE – TWO PIERS AND A STONE JETTY

Central Pier – West End Pier – Stone Jetty

CENTRAL PIER
Once the 'Taj Mahal of the North' but now just a memory

Morecambe was for a time Lancashire's second most popular resort after Blackpool and particularly found favour with the middle and working classes of West Yorkshire, who flocked to it in such numbers it was nicknamed 'Bradford-on-Sea'. Many of the essential Victorian seaside attractions of the day were erected, including theatres, a winter garden, a tower (two if you include the Warwick's Revolving Tower)

Taken from a carte-de-visite, this photograph shows Morecambe Central Pier as originally built in 1869 using components originally bound for Valparaiso in Chile.
Marlinova Collection

and two pleasure piers. The two piers, Central and West End, each once boasted wooden pavilions of the finest sort, but sadly both piers were dogged by misfortune and have been lost forever.

Having officially adopted in 1889 the name of the bay upon which it stood, Morecambe originally consisted of the three separate villages of Poulton-le-Sands, Bare and Torrisholme. Sea bathing was noted at Poulton-le-Sands around the turn of the nineteenth century and in 1829 a coach service was commenced from the Bull Hotel to Lancaster and the first regatta was held. Marine villas were erected facing Morecambe Bay to take advantage of the spectacular views of the Cumbrian Mountains. In 1848 the North Western Railway arrived at the resort and developed a harbour from where steamers ran to the Isle of Man, Fleetwood, Barrow, Furness Abbey and Blackpool. A hotel was also erected as part of the development and the general term of 'Morecambe' became increasingly used for the area.

The extension of the railway from Morecambe to the industrial towns of West Yorkshire led to it becoming the favoured resort for the residents of Bradford and Leeds in particular. In 1862, the first stretch of promenade was opened and was extended three years later with the assistance of a grant of £1,000 from the North Western Railway.

A meeting to form the Morecambe Pier Company was held at the *Kings Arms* in November 1867 and a share capital of £10,000 in 2,000 shares of £5 was announced. A bill to erect the pier was submitted in February 1868 when it was stated that a loan of £3,333 was required. After some local opposition from fishermen and the difficulties of finding a suitable site, a position for the pier opposite the Queens Hotel was chosen. The pier company then had a stroke of luck when it was able to purchase a pier that had been ordered for Valparaiso in Chile but which had failed to meet the specifications of its purchasers. The component parts of the pier had lain thereafter in crates at Liverpool Docks for two years before being purchased by the Morecambe Pier Company for only £2,500 (the iron was apparently worth £6,000). A further £3,500 was spent on erecting the 180ft wide t-shaped pier head, which was widened to 300ft in 1872. Altogether it was said that £10,000 was spent on constructing the pier to a length of 912ft.

The official opening day of the pier was Maundy Thursday, 25 March 1869. Following the ceremony on the pier, local dignitaries and officials of the Morecambe Pier Company retired to the *Kings Arms* for a celebration dinner in honour of the contractor Mr Gradwell of Barrow. The first person to use the pier was said to be a man pulling a cripple in a bath chair. However, the takings in the pier's early years amounted to around £100 per week, which was not enough to sustain the company's profitability, and in November 1871 the share capital was increased by £5,000 with the issue of 2,000 shares of £2 10s. Furthermore, in December 1878, the Morecambe Pier Company proposed borrowing on a mortgage of £3,000 to extend and strengthen the pier and add a new bandstand and dancing platform.

An early attraction on the pier was a small aquarium containing a 2ft long alligator. There were also sailings from the pier head to other Lancashire resorts, Barrow and the Isle of Man: in 1887 the vessels which used the pier included *The Roses, Sunbeam, Morecambe Queen* and *Yorkshire Lass*. The entrance fee to the pier was 1d during the day and 2d after 6p.m.; a season ticket cost 5s.

By 1886, Morecambe had around 5,000 permanent residents and 15,000 visitors during the season and during that year a horse tramway was opened along the promenade to Bare, which was extended to Heysham two years later. However, the golden age of resort attractions to be built at Morecambe was to occur during the period 1896 to 1901 when the Royalty Theatre, Victoria Pavilion (at the Winter Gardens), West End Pier, Central Pier Pavilion, Warwick Revolving Tower, Albert Hall and the Alhambra were all added. A tower was commenced in 1898 although the mere skeleton of the original elaborate design was not opened until 1909, and the resort appeared to overreach itself as buildings remained incomplete or boarded-up. Morecambe Harbour received its last commercial cargo in December 1905 having been

An Edwardian postcard of Morecambe Central Pier featuring the magnificent 'Taj Mahal of the North' pavilion opened on 11 July 1898. Marlinova Collection

140

superseded by the new harbour at Heysham. It was converted into a ship breakers yard by Thomas Ward of Sheffield which became a tourist attraction in its own right.

Tragedy struck the Central Pier on 9 September 1895 when part of the landing stage collapsed under the weight of people waiting to board the steamer *Express* for an excursion to Blackpool. Around fifty people were thrown into the sea; fortunately the tide was low and most managed to cling onto the landing stage and pier. However, three people were drowned while others sustained injuries of fractured limbs and severe lacerations.

The opening of the rival West End Pier in 1896 with its splendid domed pavilion led to the winding up of the old Morecambe Pier Company on 21 January 1897 and the formation of a new Morecambe Pier and Pavilion Company, who proposed to erect a pavilion and carry out other improvements to the now called Central Pier. The new company were incorporated on 12 February 1897 with a capital of £40,000 consisting of 30,000 ordinary shares of £1 and 10,000 preference shares and acquired the pier for £18,000. The pier was widened from 21ft to 44ft and a very attractive pavilion designed by Charles Cressey was erected and opened on 11 July 1898. Nicknamed the 'Taj Mahal of the North', the pavilion could hold up to 3,000 people and featured a concert hall with private boxes supported by nude figures, refreshment rooms, baths, an aquarium, sun decks, promenades and an observatory with telescopes. Admission to the pavilion was 6d, whilst to the pier it was 2d. The pier was further improved in 1907 with the addition of a ballroom with a roof garden adjoining the pavilion. During the winter months the pavilion and ballroom were used for roller skating.

Pierrot troupes were a feature of the entertainment provided on the Central Pier before the First World War and included The Ideals, Merry Japs, Hart's Pierrots, The Gems and The Celtics. Divers were also an attraction and included Professor Jones, Miss Rose Levere and Ted Heaton.

In 1922, the pier changed hands when it was acquired by Joseph and Herbert Proctor. They took on Jimmy Hird (father of the actress Thora Hird) as manager of the pier and in 1925 he altered the pavilion from a concert hall into a ballroom. Dancing was held three times daily at 10.30 a.m. to noon, 2.30 to 4.30 p.m. and 7 to 10 p.m. A feature of the new ballroom was a fountain situated in the middle of the floor.

One feature of the pier that Thora Hird particularly remembered was the diver Madame Rosa:

> …she had long flowing black hair and wore a bright satin bathing costume
> trimmed with sequins and legs encased in red tights, the entire ensemble hidden

tantalizingly under a red cape. She would execute the high dive mornings and afternoons according to when the tide was high. To avoid disappointment there was a board nailed on to the diving structure which displayed not only a photograph of Madame Rosa Vere in tights and sequins but also the times at which she would 'take the plunge'. I loved the entire performance and stood holding my breath hundreds of times. She would mount the diving platform and stand there with her hair blowing about and the sequins on her cape sparkling, and announce 'Ladies and gentlemen, I crave your indulgence…I shall do a high dive from this board into the open sea.' At this point she discarded her long cape and revealed all. A gasp of admiration would escape from the crowd of holiday makers, who all thought they were about to witness not only a breathtaking spectacle but a free one. They were soon enlightened however as Madame continued 'I receive no salary from the pier company, so if you will kindly show your appreciation in the usual way my assistant will pass among you, thank you.' Her assistant was her mother and who better to do the bottling? If you don't know what bottling means, its going round with a small black bag on a little wooden handle as a rule, like the Punch and Judy man does. So round her mother would go whilst Rosa stood poised on view, keeping an eye on the amount of coppers flopping into the little bag. When the bottling was over, Madame prepared to take off. Hands and arms high in the air, she would hesitate long enough for all the crowd to get the full effect and

An interior view of the Morecambe Central Pier Pavilion in the early 1930s, shortly before the building was destroyed by fire. Marlinova Collection

The destruction of the 'Taj Mahal of the North' on 31 July 1933 is vividly captured on this postcard by Webber. Marlinova Collection

Following the 1933 fire, Morecambe Central Pier was rebuilt in the popular art deco style of the time with a new pavilion, ballroom and the Dom Café. The 'New Central Pier' was opened on 16 July 1936 at a cost of £25,000. Marlinova Collection

then, whoops, off she went. As she entered the sea to a round of applause, I used to think to myself 'o how brave!' She would then swim to the pier's iron steamer landing stage, pull herself out of the mighty sea and then disappear into the rope hut, out of sight. And that was the end of the performance. Not bad for a copper coin eh?

The magnificent Taj Mahal of the North was sadly destroyed by fire on 31 July 1933. The blaze began at around 5.30 pm when smoke was seen coming from around the staging of the roller skating rink on the seaward side of the pavilion. The pier was largely deserted at the time (it was tea time in the boarding houses) and it was a woman passer-by on the promenade who phoned the fire brigade. Within half-an-hour the fire had spread to the pavilion and the famous dome was alight. Word quickly spread of the disaster and the promenade filled with onlookers. Traffic jams were caused in the town by people from Lancaster to Morecambe trying to get to see the fire. A stiff breeze blew sparks from the fire onto buildings on the promenade causing some to be set alight. The lifeboat crew ventured onto two trawlers out near the pier to fight the blaze while the bandsmen on the pier managed to rescue their two grand pianos from the pier although a leg was broken off one of them. At around 6.30 pm. Thora Hird remembered seeing *the gallant Central dome stand proud, magnificently trying to defy the flames all around its base*

An interior view of the ballroom opened on Morecambe Central Pier in 1936.
Courtesy of Richard Riding

before it collapsed into a mass of flames. The fire also destroyed 450ft of decking, six shops, bars and marble urinals: within an hour the pier had been virtually destroyed.

The Morecambe Central Pier Company could not afford to restore the pier and in 1934 it was sold to the New Central Pier Company. They rebuilt the structure in a modern art deco style in sympathy with the new Midland Hotel at a cost of £25,000 and added a new pavilion which could seat 2,000 people. The pavilion was used principally for dancing, although Neil and Claxton's Revelry's concert party was a popular feature in the late 1930s. An open air dance floor was provided on the pier deck and a floral hall was built adjoining the pavilion. Just beyond the entrance to the pier, the double-bayed Don Café was erected, also in a modernist style. The fully refurbished pier was opened to the public on 16 July 1936: the same year also saw the opening of an open air swimming pool at a time when Morecambe was at its zenith as a popular seaside resort.

The Don Café on the Central Pier however proved to be short-lived and had gone by the early 1950s. Morecambe remained busy throughout the 1950s as its manual worker customer base arrived with even more money in their pockets as wages grew. Around 80,000 people watched George Formby switch on the illuminations in 1950 and the Miss Great Britain contest at the swimming pool was nationally famous.

However, during the 1960s the resort began to sharply decline in popularity as holidaymakers jetted off to somewhere warmer and more exotic than Morecambe's out-of-date boarding houses and bad weather. The resort was described as stagnated, old-fashioned and ageing, a place where 'rigor mortis had set in'. The Central Pier took on a rather shabby air, not helped by some of the cast iron piles being encased in brick. In 1968 the Floral Hall was given over to bingo and following the McNulty brother's acquisition of the pier in 1969 the pavilion became the Miami Ballroom. However, the pier structure was in a poor shape with much of the ironwork corroded away and in 1975 it was closed after part of the decking gave way. The pier was repaired and reopened the following year but nevertheless it remained in a poor condition and was only just kept alive by its provision of wrestling, discos and amusements. The decking gave way again at Easter 1986 during a roller disco in the ballroom due to badly decayed joists and on 4 February 1987 the amusement arcade was damaged by fire, leading to the council serving a closure order.

The pier was left to decay as debates raged on about its future, an all too visible reminder of Morecambe's decline as a seaside resort. In 1989, an embarrassed Morecambe Council even left the pier off the town's

A photograph of Morecambe Central Pier in November 1985 looking rather run down and uncared for. Note the iron piles on the left encased in brick. The pier was closed as unsafe in 1987. Marlinova Collection

On 31 March 1991, a fire destroyed the pavilion and ballroom, effectively sealing the pier's fate. Demolition of the structure was carried out in 1992. Marlinova Collection

tourist map! By 1990 only 200 hotels, guest houses and self-catering units remained of 1,300 boarding houses the town had in 1956. Another fire destroyed the pavilion on 31 March 1991 and this effectively sealed the pier's fate. Despite a last minute bid to save it, demolition commenced in February 1992 and Morecambe, once a town with two piers, now had none.

WEST END PIER
A jinxed pier that suffered one storm too many

The West End of Morecambe was in many ways a separate community in its own right and its development was largely financed by Bradford businessmen: indeed one of its principal thoroughfares was called Yorkshire Street. James Erving, having acquired the land from the railway, began laying out the West End in the 1870s before it was further developed by Yorkshire-based businessmen who erected rows of bay-windowed terrace boarding houses built of Lancaster stone.

The earliest proposal for a pier in the West End was in 1878 when a 3,600ft structure was proposed by the West End Morcambe Pier Company. Fourteen years were to pass before on 18 November 1892 the Morecambe (Regent Road West End) Pier Company was formed by a consortium of Morecambe and Bradford businessmen and registered with a capital of £20,000 in £1 shares. However, at the same time, a rival company The Morecambe Alexandra Road Pier and Pavilion Company Limited were registered on 14 December 1892 with a capital of £50,000 in £1 shares for the purpose of erecting and working a promenade pier and landing stage with pavilion, concert hall, open air band kiosk, refreshment rooms, shops and lavatories. This rival scheme goaded the Regent Road Pier Company into pushing ahead with their scheme and the situation now arose where two rival companies wanted to build piers within a couple of hundred yards of each other.

In February 1893, the Board of Trade stepped in and stipulated:

> Unless the rival promoters applying for the construction of a pleasure pier and pavilion at the West End of Morecambe arrived at a mutual agreement, both applications would be thrown out on the grounds of the proposed piers intersecting with each other.

The two rival companies therefore met each other on 8 February 1893 and it was provisionally agreed the directors of the Alexandra Road Pier and Pavilion Company should take up 750 shares in the Morecambe (Regent Road West End) Pier Company on condition they withdrew their application. Eventually it was agreed the Regent Road company would pay £100 in cash towards preliminary expenses incurred by their opponents and allot them 500 fully paid-up shares, accept Mr Wood as a director and be left with a free hand regarding the appointment of an architect and engineer. The Morecambe Alexandra Road Pier and Pavilion Company were duly wound up and were dissolved on 15 September 1896.

The Royal Assent was given on 29 June 1893, on condition work on the construction of the pier was to commence within two years. Mangnall & Littlewood, the greatly respected Manchester firm of engineers, laid out plans for the finished pier to be 300 yards (900 feet) from the promenade to the pavilion and another 663 yards to the extreme end of the pier, altogether a distance of half a mile. The width of the pier to the pavilion was to be 38 feet and beyond the pavilion to the end of the pier 25 feet. The pier head widened out to 200 feet, forming a letter T, and would hold a bandstand, refreshment room and shops, and could be used as an outdoor dancing rink, as well as a landing stage for steamers. The accommodation in the pavilion could hold over 2,000 people and shops were to be located around the outside of the building.

Almost two years were indeed to pass before any work commenced on building the pier. In March 1895 the directors of the now titled West End Pier Company invited tenders for the first section of work from the promenade to the pavilion. The contract was awarded to the Widnes Iron Foundry (who were to be paid principally with shares in the pier company), in conjunction with Messrs Mayoh & Haley of London. The work began that same month and by September it was reported rapid progress was being made. The superstructure of the first section up to the pavilion was in an advanced stage, a portion of the decking had been laid down and the ornamental side railings had been commenced. Columns and girders for the erection of the pavilion were progressing, and work on the building itself, designed by J Harker, would soon be undertaken.

The formal opening of the pier took place on 3 April 1896 and was described by the *Lancaster Observer and Morecambe Chronicle*:

The Pier was formally opened by Colonel Foster MP of Hornby Castle. It is approached by a spacious bay 220 feet wide by 85 feet deep. The first section is only 900 feet up to and including the pavilion. The width of the promenade deck to the pavilion is 38 feet and altogether there is about three acres of decking. The pavilion will accommodate 2,000 people excluding the three galleries that run around three sides. The stage is 30 feet deep. The remainder of the Pier will cost £14,000 but it will not be opened yet. Around the sides of the pavilion are shelters, shops, restaurants and waiting rooms. One thousand tons of iron, 26 tons of bolts and three tons of nails have been used in the construction. Colonel Foster was presented with a beautifully chased key engraved 'Presented to Colonel Foster MP on the opening of the West End Pier, Morecambe, Easter 1896' by Mr Brown, a representative of the Widnes Iron Foundry.

The Pier Pavilion however remained to be finished and in January 1897 contracts connected with its internal decoration, furnishing and fitting were let to Messrs AR Dean of Birmingham. The work was completed by Easter and the pavilion was able to accommodate Mr E de Jong, appointed musical director for the pier orchestra for the coming season.

Following a successful summer season in 1897, preparations were made to implement the remainder of the pier. During the afternoon of 18 November 1897 the first of the 200 wooden piles for the landing stage was driven in by Mr Brown, and on 23rd April 1898 the last of the 198 piles was driven in to accommodate the pier head, which covered half an acre. In the following year, the pier was one of the first structures in the town to be installed with electric light.

With the pier now fully open and seeming set to thrive, the West End Pier Company decided to acquire a steamer of their own in a bid to gain extra revenue, so a new vessel was ordered from Gourley Bros of Dundee, to be delivered in July 1900. Christened the *Lady North*, the

Morecambe West End Pier in c.1900, two years after it was opened to its full length of 1800ft. Marlinova Collection

During a severe gale on 27 February 1903 the 1898 extension of Morecambe West End Pier was broken in two places and this postcard captures the scene at low tide. The decision was taken not to repair the damage and the extension was abandoned.
Marlinova Collection

The splendid domed pavilion of Morecambe West End Pier is captured on this postcard posted on 18 August 1906. The pavilion was designed by JD Harker and could accommodate up to 2,000 people. Marlinova Collection

A band concert on Morecambe West End c.1910. The northern side of the pavilion can be seen on the right which incorporates a café. Marlinova Collection

steamer was a twin screw steel vessel, 160 feet long, 21.1 feet in breadth and seven feet in depth, with 71 H.P.

Trips aboard the *Lady North* along the Lancashire Coast and around Morecambe Bay proved to be a popular attraction, but in 1903 disaster struck the pier and she was never able to sail from it again.

During the early hours of a particularly dark morning on Friday 27 February 1903, a severe gale blew up, which, by 8am had increased in fury with some gusts reaching up to 90mph. As high tide approached at 11am the wind was whipping the sea to such an extent the promenade was awash with water. Facing south-west meant that Morecambe often felt the full force of a prevailing wind and with tides from both north and south meeting in the bay the town was often soaked by a stormy sea at high tide. A huge crowd lined the harbour to observe the sea smashing to pieces the boulders that were meant to protect its west wall. Approaching the harbour out at sea, the SS *Brier* could be seen taking a battering from the huge waves. The steamer finally managed to dock safely, but her cargo of cattle and pigs took such a battering many of them had to be slaughtered. The lightship SS *Abbott* was not so fortunate; she sank after having broke free from her moorings.

The dramatic events of the morning continued, for shortly after the *Brier* had docked someone shouted, *the pier is rocking*. All eyes were promptly diverted in the direction of the West End Pier, whose centre portion could be seen bending to the force of the waves. The pier structure vainly held firm for a time, but with a mighty crash a section 180 feet wide broke away and drifted towards the harbour. Within a short time a further section had been demolished leaving two large gaps in the pier extension.

The damage to the pier was assessed to be between £4,000 and £5,000 and the decision was quickly taken to abandon the majority of the pier extension after a lifespan of only 4½ years. During a pier company meeting in March 1903 it was declared:

> If the structure was repaired it would be at the mercy of later storms and it is quite possible that the board of Trade would not allow the structure to be of the same strength and the cost of repair would largely add to the capital already invested in that part of the property which had never been remunerative. So it is recommended the pier head and damaged part of the extension be abandoned and plans for a new pier head on the remaining structure be discussed, the cost being about £3,500.

With the *Lady North* no longer able to use the pier, she was sold to the Morecambe Steamboat Company who sailed her from the Central Pier.

Fortunately, the jewel of the pier, its golden domed pavilion, was unaffected by the storm and continued to draw in the crowds. Popular artistes and pierrot troupes were regular features; amongst the most popular were Wallace's Pierrots, the West End Dandies, The Premiers, The Players and Miss Vera Bosisto's Orchestra of Ladies. Herr Sverdloff's Viennese Orchestra was another well-liked attraction from 1912 until the outbreak of the Great War. On warm and balmy days of summer, bands and pierrots performed on the pier deck on a little stage to the side of the pavilion.

Yet, although the pavilion was able to pay its way, the rest of the pier was proving to be highly prone to damage by stormy seas, and on the morning of Sunday 17 March 1907 it was wrecked once again. Following a month of non-stop torrential rain, a full spring tide fanned by south-westerly gales swept into a bay already full to the brim with water. Throughout the morning the gale increased in ferocity with the wind veering to the north-west. High tide was due at 8.01am but a full hour before this strong winds were sweeping huge volumes of water over the seafront. The gale reached its height at full tide, causing the water to rise sharply above its normal level. Consequently the River Lune burst its banks, leaving a mass of flooded land between Morecambe and Lancaster and a trail of wreckage, including a collapsed West End promenade and the loss of another 180 feet of the West End Pier

A postcard showing the sad scene on the morning after the pavilion on the West End Pier was burnt down during the evening of 31 May 1917. Marlinova Collection

By the 1930s, when this postcard was published, a series of disasters meant that the West End Pier looked very different from its Victorian inception. The pier's length was down to just 900ft and a series of small buildings had been erected on the site of the pavilion. Marlinova Collection

Morecambe West End Pier in the 1960s with an amusement arcade now covering the shore end of the pier. Marlinova Collection

On 11 November 1977, Morecambe West End Pier was wrecked by storms one again, this time fatally. This photograph shows people on the pier and beach looking for coins from the wrecked amusement arcade. Marlinova Collection

extension. The pier entrance was also to suffer this time when the force of the waves cracked the concrete of the pier bay and carried the pier toll offices clean away.

The pier was now beginning to appear as if it were jinxed, for it had been reduced to under half its original length within nine years. The old pier head was to remain isolated out to sea until around 1910 as a poignant reminder of the calamitous happenings to have befallen the pier. Accusing fingers were pointed at the pier company for allowing the pier to be built to an insufficient strength to withstand a gale-driven high tide. However, sadly the greatest tragedy was still to come.

On the evening of Saturday 31 May 1917, at around 10.30, the pavilion had just been emptied of a large audience following a successful evening's show when fire was spotted coming from the western end of the building and could be seen spreading rapidly. The fire brigade was quickly summoned, but it was found only one hosepipe could be brought into play and that needed to be connected to a standpipe on the promenade. To make matters worse the tide was out, so seawater was unable to be used to fight the flames and within two hours the pavilion had been completely destroyed, leaving only a huge hole in the decking where she had once stood.

The grand building was never replaced, and the pier was never quite the same again. A far smaller replacement was erected and this managed to wrest some of the audiences back from the Central Pier, whose own grand pavilion, the 'Taj Mahal of the North' was spectacularly destroyed by fire in 1933. However, by then, the West End Pier had lost the final 120ft of the extension during a storm in 1927. On 18 March 1932, the Morecambe (Regent Road West End) Pier Company went into receivership. The company was dissolved on 13 July 1934 and reconstituted as the Morecambe Marine Pier Company. The main attraction on the pier during the 1930s was the popular Cliff Shawe and his Pleasure Crew.

Following the end of the Second World War, the pier re-invented itself as a venue for open-air dancing and roller-skating, and an amusement arcade was constructed along the first third of the pier's length. The open-air dancing in particular attracted large crowds on warm, balmy summer evenings. Now in the hands of West End Pier (Morecambe and Heysham) Ltd, the attraction on the pier in 1961 was The Royal Follies, who performed in the Concert Enclosure. Refreshment facilities included the Lounge Bar, seven days fully licensed, and the Sunshine Café.

Sadly, all this came to an end during the evening of Friday 11 November 1977 when one storm too many wrecked the pier beyond repair. Over half the structure towards the shore was destroyed, leaving the open air dancing and roller skating rink stranded out in the bay. An eyewitness account spoke of horrible straining, cracking and groaning sounds as the amusement arcade slipped into the sea. On the following morning, when wind and tide had finally abated, scores of the town's youngsters could be seen scrambling amongst the mangled mess of pier ironwork and wood, and the remains of the amusement machines, hunting for cash and souvenirs.

Repair costs were estimated at £½million, far out of reach of the West End Pier Company, and demolition of the remainder of the structure was decided upon, in spite of the suggestion by a local businessman that a cable car ride be installed to link the promenade and the surviving pier 'island'. The demolition was duly carried out in 1978, though some of the intricate iron railings of the pier found their way to America while another section survives in a Morecambe back garden. That same year, David Quigley, for his First Class Honours Degree, designed a new West End Pier and the plans were printed in the press. Sadly they were not acted upon, and Morecambe West End Pier slipped away into history.

MORECAMBE STONE JETTY
A harbour pier tastefully converted into a promenade
Now used as a delightful promenade over the sea, Morecambe's Stone Jetty was originally built as part of a harbour development by the Morecambe Bay Harbour Company. Formed in 1844, the company opened a wooden jetty four years later, which handled imports of iron and iron ore from Glasgow, Whitehaven and Piel Island, Barrow-in-Furness and cattle from Ireland.

Meanwhile, parliamentary powers had been obtained in 1846 for the North Western Railway to construct a railway from Skipton to Morecambe. The line was opened on Whit Monday 1848 and was extended onto a new stone jetty at the harbour built in 1853, which featured a lighthouse, offices and waiting rooms. The railway company took over the operation of the harbour and ran steamer services to Belfast. In 1861, the jetty was connected to Hest Bank on the Lancaster to Carlisle line to enable coal to be shipped from the Yorkshire coalfields to Ireland. Pleasure trips also operated from the harbour: during the 1850s there were sailings to Barrow, Grange-over-Sands, Arnside, Fleetwood and the Isle of Man. In 1866 a service to Blackpool was commenced using the vessel *Aquilia* and then in the following year the *Queen of the Bay*. Trips also ran to the Giants Causeway and Londonderry. Following the acquisition of the North Western Railway by the Midland Railway in 1871, the majority of the shipping trade from Morecambe Harbour

A postcard captioned 'The Old Pier Morecambe 1848–1904' commemorating the period when Morecambe had its own harbour and steamer services to Ireland and the Isle of Man. The harbour was closed in 1904 upon the opening of Heysham Harbour and the pier was leased by the ship breakers, Thomas Ward. Marlinova Collection

Between 1905 and 1931 Morecambe Harbour was leased to Thomas Ward the ship breakers and a number of well-known vessels were broken up there. This aerial photograph gives a bird's eye view of the ship breaking yard. Marlinova Collection

was transferred to Fleetwood, although passenger services and the cattle trade were retained.

A description of the stone pier during the Victorian era is given in *Gorton's Official Guide to Morecambe* in 1887:

> The Stone Pier may not be inaptly described as one of the amusements for visitors; since so many of them find so much pleasure upon it. It is indeed very useful as a promenade, and many an agreeable half-hour may be spent upon it and the wooden jetty close beside it, in watching the unloading of the various vessels plying to the port of Morecambe, and in witnessing their arrival and departure. Morecambe itself is deficient in rocks, but man has supplied what nature has left out, and on the north-west side of this pier the piled up blocks of stone, resembling rocks, form the most popular resort on the whole beach for invalids and loungers, for those who like a quiet read and enjoy watching the sea in its various moods. And visitors will find these imitation rocks far more comfortable to sit upon than the real thing.

However, upon the opening of the harbour at Heysham in 1904, Morecambe Harbour became redundant and it was leased to the ship-breakers, Thomas Ward of Sheffield. Although regarded by some as a disfigurement of the seafront, Ward's became a popular tourist attraction and many visitors paid to view the doomed vessels. Some fifty-one vessels were dismantled by Wards between 1905 and 1931, which included German U boats, paddle steamers, ocean liners, battleships and a converted aircraft carrier. The full list of vessels dismantled at the harbour (reproduced from *The History of Morecambe and Heysham*) is as follows:

1905 – *Northampton* (iron frigate); *Raleigh* (sailing ship)

1906 – *Orlando* (sailing ship); *Ben-my-Chree* (paddle steamer)

1907 – *Teree* (cargo ship)

1908 – *Sophocles* (cargo ship); *Akbar* (Nelson's ironside); *Devastation* (battleship)

1909 – *Rodney* (battleship); *Benbow* (battleship)

1910 – *Centurion* (battleship); *Munchen* (battleship)

1911 – *Repulse* (battleship)

1913 – *Jet*; *Brookline*; *Nubian*; *Imperieuse*; *Pandora* (all small vessels)

1914 – *Majestic* (White Star liner that brought Crippen back from America)

1916 – *Spiraea* (oil tanker); *Berry Castle* (paddle steamer)

1918 – *Koh-i-Noor* (paddle steamer)

1919 – U boats *96*, *52* and *9*; *Trevior* (small liner); *Mona's Isle* (paddle steamer)

1920 – *Albion* (a Dardanelles monitor); *Adventure* (destroyer); *Usk* (destroyer); U boat *101*; *Kempinfelt* (battle cruiser); *Peyon* (cargo boat); *Mersey* (light cruiser); *Diadem* (light cruiser); *Ruby* (light cruiser); *217* (torpedo boat)

This 1960s postcard of Morecambe Stone Jetty features the Marineland Oceanarium opened in 1964. Marlinova Collection

During the early 1990s the stone jetty was extended and extensively refurbished as part of the TERN bird themed project which included the cormorant figure in the foreground and the floor maze behind. Marlinova Collection

1922 – *Heligoland* (German battleship)

1923 – *Edgar* (a battle cruiser known as a 'blister ship' because the lower hull was built outward as an anti-torpedo measure)

1925 – *Mexico* (liner); *Glasgow* (battle cruiser)

1926 – *Old Bebington, Norman; Coverley* (merchant vessels)

1927 – *No. 25 Hopper; Sachem* (merchant vessels)

1928 – *Cleveley; Matina* (merchant vessels)

1929 – *Admiral Ponty* (merchant vessel)

1930 – *Raphael* (cargo ship); *Tchad* (French liner)

1931 – *Pegasus* (converted aircraft carrier)

The furnishings from the doomed vessels were auctioned off and found their way into a number of Morecambe homes. The figureheads of *Northampton* and *Raleigh* were placed at the entrance to the ship-breaking yard, as was the wheel from the *Akbar*.

However, in 1932, Morecambe Council acquired the harbour from the London, Midland and Scottish Railway for £57,000 as part of their grand scheme to redevelop this area of the seafront. Wards had to vacate the Stone Jetty and it was converted into a promenade with a paddling pool, café and toilets. On the shore close to the jetty, the council erected the Band Pavilion (1933) and a huge open-air swimming pool (1936), whilst the LMS rebuilt the Midland Hotel in the favoured art deco style of the time.

A miniature zoo was later added to the jetty and in May 1964 the Marineland oceanarium was opened at a cost of £120,165. Claimed to be the first of its kind in Europe, Marineland was built by the Norwest Construction Company for Marineland (Morecambe) Limited and featured dolphin shows, children's shows and an aquarium. A further attraction was the *Moby Dick*, a three-masted schooner moored off the jetty. Unfortunately the ship was destroyed by fire in 1970 on the same day the Alhambra Theatre had its roof and top storey burnt out.

Marineland was closed and demolished when a £6 million refurbishment of the jetty and the promenade was carried out in the early 1990s. The renovation of the jetty featured a new extension and the TERN bird-themed arts project by the artist Gordon Young. Using inspiration from the bird life of Morecambe Bay, a number of cormorant sculptures were erected, and on the walkway of the jetty a floor maze, compass, tongue twisters, hopscotch and tracking games were featured. The jetty was officially reopened in June 1995 by the Agriculture Minister William Waldegrave. Later that year, the Grade II listed lighthouse and the café building were refurbished at a cost of £85,000.

CHAPTER TEN

ARNSIDE PIER

A Short but Sweet Stone Pier

Arnside was Westmorland's only seaside resort before it was incorporated into the new county of Cumbria in 1974 and is situated on the east side of Morecambe Bay. The village is sheltered under Arnside Knott and has a mixed sand and shingle beach. The place was put on the map with the building of the Ulverston and Lancaster Railway in 1853–7 and its 522 yard viaduct across the estuary of the River Kent upon which the village was situated. In 1857, a small stone pier was erected by the railway company after the building of the viaduct had restricted passage to the port at Milnthorpe. The pier replaced an earlier wooden structure. However a combination of shifting sands and silting meant it was difficult for ships to call at the pier. JA Barnes in *All Around Arnside* (1903) recorded *grass grows between the stones of its little pier, which no steamer ever approaches.* In 1897 a promenade sea wall was erected.

The small stone pier at Arnside, photographed in December 2007. The pier dates back to 1857 and is popular with fishermen. Marlinova Collection

During the early years of the twentieth century Arnside's quiet attractions were lauded in a local guide:

> The village is truly a seat of quietude and natural loveliness, a source of great health and the radiating point of charmingly picturesque drives. The botanist finds his heaven in the great variety of wild flowers and plants. The striking profusion of daffodils and lilies of the valley is a remarkable feature of the village, growing not by twos and threes but by acres, in their seasons.
>
> Boating and fishing are the principal pastimes. Accommodation is excellent in every way and good apartments, in cheery parts, are easy to secure, excepting in the height of the season in August. Arnside is very free of the rough element and its stillness is not even interrupted by a band. It is singularly the home for a month's quiet recuperation so necessary to the average business mind subject to the tension and extreme pressure of age. The sandy shore is the field for children and right heartily do they avail themselves of its advantages.
>
> It looks very pretty with its villas and cottages dotted about in the fashion of supreme watering place irregularity. Some are built on jutting crags and, seemingly, in out of the way places, while others are situated by the shore or among the narrow winding roads everywhere romantic and rich in picturesque combinations.

In 1934, a storm wrecked the end of the pier, but it was rebuilt by the London, Midland and Scottish Railway. Arnside Parish Council purchased the pier for £100 in 1964, yet it was wrecked again by another storm on 31 January 1983. Fortunately the pier was restored at a cost of £25,000 through public subscription and aid from the Countryside Commission, South Lakeland District Council, Cumbria County Council and the Frieda Scott Charitable Trust and it was reopened on 12 April 1984.

CHAPTER ELEVEN

GRANGE-OVER-SANDS BAYLEY LANE PIER AND GRANGE-OVER-SANDS CLARE HOUSE PIER (FORMERLY PIEL PIER, BARROW-IN-FURNESS)

Two wooden piers forsaken many years ago

Grange is an attractive and peaceful resort situated at the north end of Morecambe Bay close to the Lake District. Originally situated in Lancashire 'O'er the Water' it was transferred to the new county of Cumbria in 1974.

The pier at the foot of Bayley Lane, Grange-over-Sands c.1900. The pier was largely unused by this time and would shortly be demolished. Marlinova Collection

Grange-over-Sands Clare House Pier c.1910, originally situated at Piel, Barrow-in-Furness. The pier came to Grange in the 1890s, but was badly damaged by a storm in 1928. Marlinova Collection

The beautiful situation of the town began to attract visitors in the first quarter of the nineteenth century and it acquired a reputation as a 'good sea bathing village' boasting a healthy climate. Coaches from Lancaster to Ulverston ran over the sands of Morecambe Bay at low tide and called at Grange on the way. However this traffic virtually ceased with the opening of the Furness Railway in 1857 between Lancaster and Ulverston which included a station at Grange. The railway company erected the Grange Hotel in 1866 and also the first stretch of promenade.

In 1867 a visitor wrote in the *Westmorland Gazette*:

It is the character of a sanatorium that Grange is growing and will flourish. It is not fast or boisterous nor overcrowded like some places one might name: it has neither bathing vans or donkeys. A guide to Grange published in 1891 pointed out its high reputation for respectability and dignified response. This is not a paradise of burnt-cork artists, of German bands, of galloping and reckless trippers, it is not in fact a bathing-place in the ordinary sense.

Further extensions of the promenade, most notably in 1902–4, was paid for by Harold Porritt JP, a textile factory director who came to live in the town in 1895. He generously also provided a tea room on the promenade and a bandstand, whilst his cousin Lt Col AT Porritt helped contribute towards the cost of extensions to the parks and gardens.

Grange's first pier was erected by the Morecambe Bay Steamboat Company at the foot of Bayley Lane in 1875, replacing a small jetty. This was joined by another wooden pier built adjoining Clare House by Richard Bush in 1893.

The Clare House pier had been constructed using timber from an 810ft pier originally situated at Piel, Barrow-in-Furness. This had been authorised in 1843 for John Abel Smith, the proprietor of Roa Island who hoped that the Furness Railway would use his pier for iron ore traffic. However following a dispute over tolls, the iron ore traffic went to Barrow. Nevertheless the Furness Railway made arrangements with the Preston & Wyre Railway to provide a steamer service from Fleetwood to Piel Pier to connect with the Furness Railway passenger service, which commenced in 1846.

The service from Piel proved to be fairly intermittent at first and for a period in 1847 it was transferred to Barrow. The service returned to Piel in May 1848 and eventually the Furness Railway bought out Smith's interests there. They commenced a regular service from the pier in 1852, although it was closed for a period in the following year due to storm damage.

On 6 June 1861, the Furness and Midland railways joint line was opened from Wennington to Carnforth, giving the Midland Railway access to Barrow. The Barrow Steam Navigation Company (involving the Furness Railway, Midland Railway and James Little & Co) was formed to operate the Midland's Isle of Man and Belfast steamers and on 1 July 1861 the Douglas service was transferred to Piel Pier, as were the Belfast sailings from 2 September.

Piel Pier continued to remain in railway use until 1881 when, following the opening of Ramsden Dock and the provision of a new railway station, the Isle of Man boats were transferred to the dock on 1 June. The transfer of the Belfast service followed suit in October.

The pier remained in irregular use for small craft until it was dismantled in 1891 and part of it was re-erected at Grange. The Clare House Pier as it was termed largely superseded the Bayley Lane Pier, which became derelict. In 1900, there was a mention of the Grange Pier and Baths Company putting the Bayley Lane Pier in good order but it was demolished in the early years of the twentieth century. Steamer trips from Morecambe aboard the *Yorkshire Lass* and *Morecambe Queen* used both piers although they were only available at high tide.

In 1899, detailed plans were made for a garden city at Grange on reclaimed land beyond Meathop Marsh. Some 666 houses, designed by Boulton & Paul, were to be served by a gas works, railway station and Marine Parade. A six-roomed wood framed house was to have cost £730, but an abnormally high tide in 1907 flooded the ground for several weeks and the plan was abandoned.

Steamer sailings ceased to the Clare House Pier around 1910 as it became increasingly difficult for the larger craft to use it: the *Sunbeam* was the last vessel to call. This was largely down to a shifting of the channels in the bay, started by the building of the viaduct and causeway to Holme Island. Small pleasure boats continued to use the pier until it was badly damaged by a storm on 28 October 1928. The shore end of the pier survived for a time as a slipway but has now disappeared. A plaque commemorating Grange's two piers can be seen at the site of the Bayley Lane Pier.

CHAPTER TWELVE

SILLOTH PIER

A Vanished Wooden Harbour Pier popular for a Stroll

The small Cumbrian seaside resort of Silloth was developed by the Carlisle and Silloth Bay Railway Dock and Company in the 1850s to provide a deep water dock to serve Carlisle. Previously, Carlisle had been served by an eleven mile canal opened in 1823 that ran to Fishers Cross, which had been renamed Port Carlisle. However, by the 1850s, the canal was silting up in the upper reaches of the Solway Firth and could no longer accommodate large enough vessels to supply the city. The canal was closed in 1853 and was converted into a railway to continue to serve the diminishing traffic calling at Port Carlisle.

In 1855, the Silloth Dock Act was passed, authorising a thirteen mile branch railway to leave the Port Carlisle line at Drumburgh and head south along the coast to a sparsely populated farming hamlet called Silloth where Admiralty surveys had established that there was relatively

Although built as a harbour arm and for commercial use, Silloth Pier was a popular promenade for visitors to the resort. Marlinova Collection

deep water close offshore. The Act also allowed for the construction of a pier and dock fitted with gates to retain water at low tide to keep ships afloat.

Work began on the railway and dock in August 1855 and within twelve months the railway had reached Silloth. A 1,000ft long timber piled pier was erected at the dock and this was usable by shipping in the summer of 1857. The dock was officially opened on 3 August 1859 and was formally named Marshall Dock in honour of the local Member of Parliament who was a major shareholder in the Carlisle & Silloth Bay Dock and Railway Company.

Regular freight services were established from Silloth to Liverpool, Ireland and the Isle of Man transporting cotton, coal, livestock, timber, slate and phosphate fertilisers. A local passenger and freight service also ran across the Solway Firth to Annan, Dumfries and Carsethorn. The dock and railway passed to the North British Railway Company who expanded the service. However during a storm on 6 April 1879 the dock entrance and gates were wrecked, trapping about twenty vessels in the dock. Temporary repairs were affected until the more sheltered New Dock was opened in June 1885. The volume of trade through the new dock was increased with the opening of a flour mill alongside the dock, resulting in large volumes of wheat being imported. The trade in coal and cattle with Ireland remained buoyant.

Silloth also had a second identity as a small health-giving resort and a bathing establishment and machines were provided. The long wooden pier built at the entrance to the dock was used for promenading and fishing by visitors and locals and as a base for boat trips. By the 1920s however the sea end of the pier was subsiding and the sections at the sea end began intermittently falling into the sea. The last surviving 100ft section was demolished in 1973 and was replaced by a short groyne and rubble breakwater, built to try and prevent the dock entrance from being silted up by the northward drift of beach material.

The railway to Silloth was eventually felled by Beeching's Axe in 1964 but the dock remains busy. Now in the hands of Associated British Ports, the trade through Silloth includes wheat from Europe and North America and a variety of agribulks from Russia. A small local shrimping fleet also operates from the outer dock.

CHAPTER THIRTEEN

DOUGLAS IRON PIER

Long Demolished to be used Elsewhere

The gateway to the Isle of Man, Douglas, with its fine sweep of a bay, grew as a fashionable seaside resort during the nineteenth century and was easily accessible by ship from the Lancastrian coast. The growth of the town can be traced back to the mid-seventeenth century when the harbour became handily placed for trade between the merchants of the isle and those of Liverpool. The formation of the Douglas Town Commissioners in 1860 led to rapidly expanding developments of the harbour and resort facilities that saw the town become the isle's official capital in 1869.

The town's first seafront promenade was erected in 1864 by Samuel Harris, the last High Bailiff of Douglas. In 1868, he granted it to the Town Commissioners who renamed it the Harris Promenade. The previous

The Iron Pier at Douglas c.1880s, so called to distinguish it from the Victoria landing pier. Erected in 1869, the pier was an early casualty and was dismantled in 1894. Iron from the structure was used to build Rhos-on-Sea Pier in north Wales. Marlinova Collection

A very rare view of the walkway of Douglas Iron Pier c.1870, taken from a carte-de-visite. A notice on the railings directs 'keep to the right'. Marlinova Collection

year had seen the foreshore acquired from the Crown for £764 and the Loch Promenade was laid out and imposingly lined with properties designed by WJ Rennison. The Victoria Pier was started in 1867 to handle the town's shipping traffic and parts of the old slum areas were swept away to enable imposing terraces, many housing hotels and boarding houses for visitors, to be laid out in the upper and lower areas of the town. By 1870, 60,000 visitors were arriving annually, principally from the north-west of England.

The great development of promenade piers at English and Welsh resorts had begun to gather pace during the 1860s and as the growth of Douglas blossomed during the later half of the decade a group of local businessmen were keen for the provision of a pleasure pier for both locals and visitors.

Situated in the centre of Douglas Bay at the foot of Broadway, the foundation stone for the Iron Pier (as it was known to distinguish it from the Victoria landing pier) was laid in January 1869. John Dixon served as both engineer and contractor (although Waynman Dixon supervised the work) and the pier took only six months to construct at a cost of £6,000. On 19 August 1869, it was officially opened by Mrs HB Loch, wife of the Lieutenant-Governor of the Isle of Man.

The pier was 1,000ft in length and was supported on thirty-nine pairs of cast iron piles, upon which rested wrought iron girders overlaid with a timber deck. The width of the structure was 17ft, opening out to 40ft at the head. A broad flight of steps at the entrance led to a toll house resembling a small Chinese pagoda. A refreshment room was placed on the pier head with a smoking gallery on the roof and the pier also had a camera obscura for a time, which was later relocated to Douglas Head. Steamers could use the pier head at all states of the tide. The pier also formed the demarcation line between the ladies bathing ground to the north and that of the gentlemen to the south.

The delights of the pier were featured in a poem written by James Middleton Sutherland in July 1873, included in *Douglas and other poems:*

The Douglas Iron Pier
HERE stands in lovely Douglas Bay,
An Iron Pier, so grand for walking,
Where hundreds promenade every day,
So gaily dressed and lively talking.

But chief at eve, at eight about,
After th' arrival of the steamers,
The Pier looks best, for then come out
The ladies decked with flowers and streamers.

And sweet it is these belles to see
Of Mona's Isle and other places,
All promenading in their glee,
With beaming eyes, and oh! what faces!

The aptest language ne'er could tell
The beauties of these charming creatures,
So fair, they seem to have a spell,
They have such pleasing forms and features.

The scenery around is grand,
The sea beneath which rolls in glory
Is clear as crystal, and the sand
Is bright, as in a fairy story.

The wavelets murmur as they flow
To kiss the pebbly shore so golden,
While fresh'ning Zephyrs softly blow
Around us, as in days of olden.

Upon the waters, deeply blue,
Glide the little boats so lightly;
While on the distant hills, a hue
Of richest purple rests so brightly.

On summer eves musicians play,
The people here all love romancing,
Which makes them animated, gay,
Tho' here is not permitted dancing.

When Evening round her mantle throws,
And shines the Moon upon the ocean,
When all is steeped in calm repose,
And not a wave appears in motion,

'Tis sweet to sit when all is still,
And watch the pale Moon sailing o'er us,
And think of those we love, until
The future brightly lies before us.

The pier's admission charge in 1874 was 1d; 1s 6d a month or 5s per annum. However, the pier was never a great success financially. The pier's distance away from the hub of the town around the Victoria Pier was a discouragement to some, whilst others were happy to benefit from the free promenading and view of the shipping obtained from the Victoria Pier. The simple charms of the Iron Pier began to be particularly forsaken from the 1880s in favour of the resort's large entertainment venues that were springing up. Beginning with the building of the Derby Castle complex in 1877, Douglas became over-rich with the provision of great ballrooms, theatres and music halls, which included the Falcon Cliff Pavilion (1887, demolished 1896), Grand Theatre (1888, with music hall, swimming baths and bowling alley), Palace Ballroom (1889, an opera house was added in 1894), Belle Vue Pleasure Gardens (1892), Empire Theatre (1893), and Marina Theatre (1895, restyled by Frank Matcham as the Gaiety Theatre and Opera House in 1900).

With the pier failing to pay its way, it was put up for sale in 1893. A number of offers for it from resorts in England and Wales wanting to erect their own pier were expressed, but eventually the pier was sold to a group of businessmen from the Welsh resort of Rhos-on-Sea. They dismantled the pier in 1894 and used the iron from it to erect their own pier (which was longer than Douglas), opened in April 1895. The pier head refreshment room did not go to Rhos but was moved to Groudle, where it was used as G Dobie's refreshment rooms for many years.

CHAPTER FOURTEEN

RAMSEY QUEENS PIER

A Fine Pier with an Uncertain Future

Ramsey's fine iron pier was built to provide a safe berthing point for steamers at all states of the tide and was promoted by the Ramsey Harbour Commissioners, with financial assistance of £6,000 also being provided by the Ramsey Town Commissioners. The design of Sir John Goode CE and the tender of £36,710 submitted by contractors Head, Wrightson of Stockton-on-Tees were chosen.[35] The pier was to be 2,160ft long and for the most part was 21ft 3in wide, except where the width of the pier was widened for five pairs of seating bays. The structure consisted of a timber deck supported on wrought iron girders and cruciform wrought iron supporting piles encased in cast iron legs. These

The Yorks and Lancs disembarking at Ramsey Pier in 1907. This fine structure was opened in 1886 and had been extended to 2,248ft between 1899 and 1901 with the addition of a two-tier landing stage. Marlinova Collection

The Wickham railcar at the pier head on Ramsey Pier c.1960: this had been added to the pier's 3ft gauge tramway stock in 1950. The pier head building had an identical twin on Herne Bay Pier, built by the same contractor. Marlinova Collection

were placed in rows of three at 40ft centres, with the outer two columns raked at an angle, although five double rows of columns were used to support the seating bays. A landing stage was to be provided on the south side of the pier.

Work began in June 1882 and the pier was officially opened as the Queens Pier on 22 July 1886 by Rowley Hill, the Bishop of Sodor and Man having cost £40,752 to eventually build. A 3ft gauge tramway used in the construction of the pier was retained for use as a baggage line using seven four-wheeled trucks and one wagon propelled by hand.

The pier received 159 passenger steamers during its first year of operation. The principal steamer operator to use the pier was the Isle of Man Steam Packet Company, whose most famous vessel was the SS *Mona's Queen*. Built in 1885, she remained in service until 1929 by which time she was the last paddle steamer in the company's fleet. However, it soon became clear that the pier's landing stage was inadequate and in 1893 construction of a new east berth was approved. In 1899, a new two-level landing stage was opened, extending the pier to 2,248ft, although the work was not completed until 1901. At the same time a hand-propelled passenger car was purchased.

The Planet locomotive and toast rack car by the entrance to Ramsey Pier c.1960, which had been introduced in 1937. Marlinova Collection

Ramsey Pier in 2000, which has been largely closed to the public since June 1991 as debates rage on about its future. Marlinova Collection

Although used principally as a landing stage for boats, the pier did provide some concessions to entertainment. Band concerts were sometimes held on the roof of the pier head café and there were swimming demonstrations.

In 1902, the pier was honoured with a royal visit when King Edward VII landed there. King George V and Queen Mary also used it during their visit to the island in July 1920.

The pier tramway's hand-propelled car was replaced in 1937 by a Planet petrol locomotive, which pulled a toast rack carriage seating ten. In 1950 the Isle of Man Harbour Board added a Wickham railcar that was powered by a Ford V8 petrol engine. Six years later the pier entrance acquired a plain concrete building that did nothing to enhance its appearance, although the original kiosks remained in situ.

However, on 10 September 1970, steamer calls at the pier ceased due to the poor condition of the wooden berthing head. The last vessel to call was the *Manxman* on the Belfast service. The landing stage was fenced off in 1979 and two years later on, 9 September 1981, the tramway was closed by its operators the Manx Electric Railway Society. The pier remained open for promenading and for anglers but suffered from vandalism, and in 1991 the charming pier head café was destroyed by fire. This was replaced by a new shelter with toilets, which within days of opening were also vandalised. These acts, along with concerns about the pier's safety led to it being closed in June 1991, although until 2003 it was allowed to be used for special open days. A 'Friends of Ramsey Queens Pier' was formed in 1994 and in the following year the pier was placed on the Manx register of protected buildings.

The pier remains closed as the debate rages on about what to do with it. In 2007, a Council of Ministers Working Group issued a questionnaire to 1,800 homes in Ramsey and 1,400 elsewhere on the island asking for their views on whether the pier should be restored and how. Of the 46% who responded, 81% were in favour of some type of heritage restoration of the pier, although 10% of these would not be in favour of the pier being linked to a new marina project. The Friends of Ramsey Pier continue to push hard for this listed structure to be restored and it is hoped they succeed in their endeavour. The pier is an excellent surviving example of a largely unaltered Victorian iron pier and the finest surviving work of Head, Wrightson, the premier constructors of seaside piers. The Planet locomotive and trailer are now cared for by the Isle of Man Railway & Tramway Preservation Society.

CHAPTER FIFTEEN

THE PIERS THAT NEVER WERE

Piers Proposed but Never Built

AINSDALE

In 1878 Thomas Weld-Blundell formed the Freshfield Pier and Land Company to the south of Ainsdale, but the scheme never got off the ground. A further proposal was forwarded by his son, Charles Weld-Blundell, who formed the Ainsdale-on-Sea Land and Pier Company. This was registered on 13 December 1900 with a capital of £10,000 in £1 shares and envisaged a promenade that would run for six miles from Birkdale to Freshfield, with Ainsdale at its centre that would include a pier, large hotels and a boating lake. A railway station was opened on the Southport & Cheshire Lines Railway (known as 'Seaside') in 1901 and a hotel was built adjoining it, yet progress in laying out the new town proved to be painfully slow due to a lack of interest in the scheme (by 1906 only 359 of the shares had been taken up). A revised plan for the seafront prepared by FG Fraser, a Liverpool architect, for Well-Blundell in 1906 dropped the pier. The Ainsdale-on-Sea Land and Pier Company was finally dissolved in 13 March 1917 but had effectively ceased operating some ten years earlier.

BIRKDALE

The Southport and Birkdale Crescent Pier was proposed but quickly foundered without an Act of Parliament being gained.

BLACKPOOL PALATINE

Promoted in 1898, this was to have been a 650ft long pier with a broad deck housing a vast range of amusement facilities, including a winter garden, concert hall and fairground rides. With three piers in the resort already, this plan had little chance of getting off the ground.

BLACKPOOL SEAWATER

This was to have been a small promenade pier built in conjunction with a scheme to bring seawater ashore to supply hotels and bathing establishments. Once again, local opposition by both residents and the corporation killed the plan.

GRANGE-OVER-SANDS
A proposal to build a pier in 1885 by the Grange Pier and Baths Company soon floundered.

HOYLAKE
A pier of 200ft was proposed for this quiet Wirral resort, but the Act of Parliament was never passed. A small jetty was erected instead in 1902.

MORECAMBE ALEXANDRA ROAD
In the latter part of 1892, there were two rival schemes to build a pier for the rapidly developing West End of Morecambe. Following the formation of the Morecambe (Regent Road West End) Pier Company on 18 November 1892, the rival Morecambe Alexandra Road Pier and Pavilion Company was registered on 14 December 1892 with a capital of £50,000 in £1 shares.

The Alexandra Road Company intended to build a promenade pier and landing stage with pavilion, concert hall, open air band kiosk, refreshment rooms, shops and lavatories. However in February 1893, the Board of Trade insisted that they would only agree to the construction of one pier. The two companies met and it was decided that the Alexandra Road Company would withdraw their application and take up shares in the Regent Road Company. The Morecambe Alexandra Road Pier and Pavilion Company were duly wound-up and were eventually dissolved on 15 September 1896.

MORCAMBE (WEST END)
The earliest proposal for a pier in the West End was in 1878 when a 3,600ft structure was proposed by the West End Morcambe Pier Company.

SOUTHPORT ALEXANDRA
The Southport Alexandra Pier and Arcade Company was incorporated on 4 December 1866 with a capital of £60,000 consisting of £12,000 shares of £5 each. The company was to allocate £15,000 to build a pier of around 4500ft, claiming the existing pier was inadequate, and the rest was to be spent on providing shops, concert halls, assembly rooms and other attractions in the vicinity of Lord Street. The proposed pier was endorsed by the Board of Trade, but the House of Commons rejected its parliamentary bill in March 1867, probably because the operating company of the existing pier promised to carry out improvements. Based at Kings Chambers, 2 East Bank Street, Southport, the Southport Alexandra Pier and Arcade Company was formally dissolved on 31 August 1883.

POSTSCRIPT

The restoration of Southport Pier and the perceived viabilities of the three Blackpool piers should ensure the continuing presence of pleasure piers on the Lancashire coast. The bright new Southport Pier with its stylish tram and contemporary pavilion has assumed the mantle of number one Lancashire pier from a rather tired looking Blackpool North. Make no mistake, the North Pier remains one of the finest piers in the land, but in recent years the peeling paint is more evident, the tram has gone and the future of live entertainment on the pier has been cast into doubt.

The charm of the North Pier has always lain in its traditional Victorian appeal of the open promenade deck, delightful kiosks, the end of the pier show and sun lounge organist. As Blackpool looks towards the future, whether as a traditional seaside resort or gambling mecca, we can only hope that the identity of North Pier will not be sacrificed for another fairground or amusement arcade. They already reign on the somewhat soulless Central and South piers.

Lancashire's other surviving pier, St Annes, continues on its merry unassuming way. The pier's lovely under-deck ironwork and unique entrance building ensures that it remains a structure of interest, even if not a totally satisfying one. The sole purpose of the pier now is as a covered amusement arcade. What remains of the open promenade deck is rarely available to the public, seemingly because it makes no money and two charming kiosks which were situated at the end of the truncated pier have been removed. However, arguably, an amusement arcade pier is better than no pier at all.

The future of Ramsey Pier, the sixth survivor of the twelve fully-fledged pleasure piers that graced the north-west coast, continues to remain in doubt. Long closed and decaying by the year, it can only be hoped that something is done to ensure the future of this fine pier before it is too late.

Southport has shown that piers can remain the focal point of a resort's regeneration as they were when they were conceived in that golden Victorian age. Here's to a future with piers.

NOTES

1. Designated a royal highway, the ferry crossing between Liverpool and Birkenhead is still marked by crowns on the gangway posts at Woodside and Liverpool Pier Head.
2. *Waterlily* was one of three 'flower' boats introduced by Wallasey in 1862. The others were *Mayflower* and *Wild Rose*.
3. The Palace boasted the largest plunge baths in the country by 1896, but a big wheel planned for the site in that year was not built. The Palace Theatre started showing films in 1906 but was demolished in 1933 following fire damage in 1916. However, the amusement park on the site flourished and an art deco influenced amusement arcade was erected by the Wilkie family just prior to the Second World War. The Wilkie's continue to operate the park at the present time.
4. The Winter Garden was redesigned as a theatre/cinema in 1931 but was converted into a bingo hall in 1957. The building was demolished in 1991 after lying derelict for a number of years.
5. The Tivoli was demolished in 1978 after suffering fire damage two years earlier.
6. Both the *Iris* and *Daffodil* were requisitioned as troop ships during the First World War and saw service during the naval raid on Zeebrugge on 23 April 1918. On their return to the Mersey they were granted the Royal prefix in recognition of their service.
7. Mother Redcaps was demolished in 1974 but is commemorated in the name of the retirement flats built on the site.
8. The old Seacombe Ferry Hotel was demolished during the reclaiming of the bay. The second hotel was itself replaced in 1978 by a smaller pub/restaurant.
9. In 1947 a radar scanner was installed on top of the clock tower to guide the ferries across the river.
10. Her service on the Mersey was ended in 1991 when she was sold for use as a floating nightclub on the Thames. She was the last of the old Wallasey vessels to remain on the river, the *Leasowe* having been withdrawn in 1974, *Egremont* in 1975 and *Royal Daffodil II* in 1977.
11. Under the Mersey Tunnel Act of 1925 the Mersey Tunnel Joint Committee were to be responsible for financial control of the Birkenhead ferries (thus safeguarding the ratepayers from any losses) for a period of twenty-one years from the opening of the tunnel.
12. Financial assistance from the Mersey Tunnel Joint Committee finally ceased

on 17 July 1974 upon the 40th anniversary of the opening of the first Mersey Tunnel.

13. The vessel was eventually scraped in 1898.

14. The Refreshment Rooms were commonly known as 'Donovan's' after long time licensee John Donovan, who was there from the 1870s to 1903.

15. According to a Birkenhead Corporation report in 1909, the original landing stage of 1865 was apparently replaced by a larger structure in 1870.

16. The Eastham Ferry Hotel was greatly rebuilt in 1846 by the local landowner Sir Thomas Stanley.

17. The £50,000 capital consisted of 5,000 £5 preference shares (with a 7% dividend) and £25,000 £1 ordinary shares.

18. The profit/loss figures for the years 1910-1913 were July 1910-January 1911 loss of £811; January-July 1911 profit of £1603; July 1911-January 1912 loss of £1491; January-July 1912 loss of £408; July 1912-January 1913 loss of £1612.

19. The toll was abolished in 1859 when the Southport Improvement Commissioners took over the promenade. They carried out further extensions to the promenade in 1873 (southwards to Duke Street) and 1881 (northwards to Park Road).

20. The Opera House, designed by Frank Matcham, was added to the Winter Gardens complex in 1891 but was destroyed by fire in 1929: it was replaced by the Garrick Theatre. The Winter Garden was demolished in 1933 and the Pavilion, having been used as a cinema, in 1962.

21. The fairground was relocated to Princes Park near Marine Drive in 1922 and became known as Pleasureland. The park was leased by the Blackpool Pleasure Beach Company but closed in 2006. A smaller park known as New Pleasureland currently occupies the site until it is redeveloped.

22. Lytham Hall was acquired by the town in 1997 with the help of British Aerospace and is open to the public at weekends.

23. The windmill was erected in 1805 and worked until fire destroyed the machinery in 1919. Restored by Fylde Borough Council it is now used as a Tourist Information Centre. Adjoining the windmill is the lifeboat station erected in 1854 and now a lifeboat museum.

24. The St Annes Hotel was demolished in 1985 and the site redeveloped as the St Annes Tavern, shops and a car park.

25. Maxwell had been appointed agent of the St Annes Hotel Company but resigned in November 1877.

26. Sited opposite the South (later Central Pier), the Wellington was later combined with Wylie's South Pier Hotel but was demolished in 1904.

27. Amongst the amusements provided at Uncle Tom's Cabin was an open air theatre, dancing platform, refreshment stalls (including a beer house), a switchback railway, camera obscura and J Wright's American Portraits.

Severe erosion of the cliffs led to some of the buildings tumbling down on to the beach below, and on 4 October 1907 Uncle Tom's Cabin was closed. A new public house bearing the same name was opened further inland.

28. Blackpool was incorporated as a borough on 21 January 1876.

29. The North Pier Steamship Company (Blackpool) was incorporated on 1 February 1895 with a capital of £40,000 divided into £4,000 shares of £10. On 11 December 1900, the capital was increased to 60,000. They went into liquidation on 11 April 1905 and were wound up on 18 March 1907.

30. The Palace was sadly demolished in 1961-2 to make way for a John Lewis department store.

31. The illuminations were revived in 1925 to extend the holiday season into the autumn. Lord Derby performed the first celebrity switch on in 1934.

32. He received a knighthood in 1838.

33. Hesketh had originally intended to develop a new town on the banks of the River Wyre near Thornton to be called 'Wyreton'.

34. The dock was extended in 1871 and a grain elevator was added in 1882.

35. However, it also appears that Head, Wrightson also had significant input into the design of the pier. The structure resembles their piers at Skegness and Herne Bay and the building erected at the end of the pier is identical to that provided at Herne Bay.

ACKNOWLEDGEMENTS

The author wishes to thank the following for their kind assistance in the preparation of this book:

Linda Sage for her research assistance, Paul Grant and Patricia Herbert for proofreading, Wilf Watters, Richard Riding, National Piers Society, The National Archives at Kew, British Library Newspapers at Colindale.

BIBLIOGRAPHY OF
REFERENCE SOURCES

General

http://www.engineering-timelines.com

http://www.wikipedia.com

Illustrated London News (various issues)

Piers of the Realm, Robin Johnson (Complimentary Studies Thesis, 1976)

Seaside Piers, Simon Adamson (BT Batsford, 1977)

The English Seaside Resorts: A Social History 1750–1914, John K Walton (St Martins Press, 1983)

Pavilions on the Sea: The History of the Seaside Pleasure Pier, Cyril Bainbridge (Robert Hale, 1986)

Wakes Seaside Resorts, Ron Freethy (Faust Publishing, 1986)

Wonderlands by the Waves: A History of the Lancashire Seaside Resorts, John K Walton (Lancashire County Books 1992)

The Bass Railway Trips, Rod Pearson (Breedon Books, 1993)

The Lancashire Wakes Holidays, Robert Poole (Lancashire County Books, 1994)

Piers Railways & Tramways, Keith Turner (Oakwood Press 1999)

Wakey! Wakey! Lancashire Trips and Treats, Catherine Rothwell (Enigma Publishing, 2003)

Yorkshire's Seaside Piers, Martin Easdown (Wharncliffe Books, 2008)

Piers: The Journal of the National Piers Society (various issues)

River Mersey Piers

National Archives: CRES 37/64 New Brighton

National Archives: CRES 37/65 New Brighton

National Archives: CRES 37/66 New Brighton

National Archives: CRES 37/232 New Brighton

National Archives: CRES 37/359 New Brighton

National Archives: MT10/210 New Brighton

National Archives: MT10/911 New Brighton

National Archives: MT48/35 New Brighton

National Archives: MT76/54 New Brighton

National Archives: CRES 37/242 Egremont

National Archives: CRES 37/243 Egremont

National Archives: CRES 37/832 Egremont

National Archives: CRES 37/1388 Egremont

National Archives: CRES 37/1979 Egremont

National Archives: CRES 58/985 Egremont

National Archives: MT10/518 Egremont

National Archives: MT/1459 Egremont

National Archives: BT31/1809/6950 Tranmere

National Archives: MPE1/644 Tranmere

National Archives: MT10/499 Tranmere

National Archives: CRES 58/995 Rock Ferry

National Archives: CRES 37/16 New Ferry

National Archives: CRES 37/806 New Ferry

National Archives: CRES 58/993 New Ferry

National Archives: MR1/1601 New Ferry

National Archives: BT31/7507/53458 Eastham

National Archives: MT10/1454 Eastham

National Archives: RAIL 112/3 Eastham

Mersey Ferries Volume 1 – Woodside to Eastham, TB Maund (Transport Publishing Company, 1991)

Mersey Ferries Volume 2 – The Wallasey Ferries, TB Maund and Martin Jenkins (Black Dwarf Publications, 2003)

West Coast Steamers, Duckworth and Langmuir (T Stephenson & Sons, 1966)

Castles in the Sand, Maurice G Hope (GW & A Hesketh, 1982)

Yesterday's Wirral No. 4: Wallasey and New Brighton, Ian and Marilyn Boumphrey (authors, 1986)

Yesterday's Wirral No. 5: Wallasey, New Brighton and Moreton, Ian and Marilyn Boumphrey (authors, 1988)

Sandstone and Mortar: More of Old Wallasey, Noel E Smith (author, 1992)

The Inviting Shore: A Social History of New Brighton Part One 1830–1939, Anthony M Miller (Countywise Limited, 1996)

Rock Ferry, New Ferry and Bebington, Dave Mitchelson (Sigma Press, 1998)

The Changing Years by Rock Ferry Local History (Wirral Metropolitan College, 1991)

Yesterday's Wirral No. 9: Ellesmere Port to Bromborough, Ian and Marilyn Boumphrey (authors, 1999)

Yesterday's Wirral Pictorial History 1890–1953, Ian and Marilyn Boumphrey (authors, 2000)

Cross the Mersey: 850 Years of the World-Famous Ferries, Arabella McIntyre-Brown and Guy Woodland (Garlic Press Publishing Ltd, 2003)

Yesterday's Birkenhead, Ian Boumphrey (author, 2007)

Yesterday's Wallasey and New Brighton, Ian Boumphrey (author, 2008)

Wigan Pier

National Archives: RAIL 1007/274

Wigan Pier: An Illustrated History, John Hannavy and Jack Winstanley (Smiths Books (Wigan) Ltd, 1985)

Southport Pier

National Archives: BT31/31321/39465

National Archives: BT41/645/3529

National Archives: MT6/1326/3

National Archives: MT10/1766

North Moels and Southport: A History, Peter Aughton (Carnegie Publishing, 1988)

Southport in old picture postcards, Philip Mayer and George Openshaw (SB Publications, 1989)

Southport through the Letter Box: A Picture Postcard History of Southport, GA and AG Burgess (GB Studios, 1990)

Southport Stage and Screen, Harold Ackroyd (author, 1991)

Southport in Focus, Catherine Rothwell (Printwise Publications, 1991)

A History of Southport, FA Bailey (Sefton Council Arts and Libraries, 1992)

Southport: A Pictorial History, Harry Foster (Phillimore, 1995)

Southport in old photographs, Jack Smith (Alan Sutton, 1995)

Southport, Ian Simpson (Tempus Publishing, 1996)

Back to the Sea: The True Story of Southport, Frank Bamford (author, 2001)

Lytham and St Annes Piers

National Archives: BT31/839/730C Lytham Pier

National Archives: BT31/5014/33610 Lytham Pier

National Archives: BT31/15540/46010 Lytham Pier

National Archives: MT10/580 Lytham Pier

National Archives: MT81/205 St Annes Pier

Lytham Times

Rage of Sand, Gabriel Harrison (Ernest Benn Limited, 1971)

Lytham St Annes in old picture postcards, Kathleen Eyre (European Library, 1983)

Years of Piers: Memories of St Annes Pier on its Centenary (Handbook Publishing, 1985)

Lytham and St Annes: The Reluctant Resorts, Kath Brown (Lancashire County Books, 1992)

Lytham St Annes in old photographs, Catherine Rothwell (Alan Sutton, 1993)

Sand Grown: The Lytham St Annes Story, Kathleen Eyre (Landy Publishing, 1999)

Lytham St Annes: A Pictorial History, RA Haley (Phillimore, 1995)

Images of Lytham St Annes, Steve Singleton (Breedon Books, 2005)

St Annes on the Sea: A History, Peter Shakeshaft (Carnegie Publishing, 2008)

Blackpool North, Central and South Piers

National Archives: BT31/615/2582 Blackpool North Pier

National Archives: BT31/6099/43183 Blackpool North Pier

National Archives: CRES 37/143 Blackpool North Pier

National Archives: MT10/255 Blackpool North Pier

National Archives: MT10/260 Blackpool North Pier
National Archives: MT10/730 Blackpool North Pier
National Archives: CRES 37/146 Blackpool Central Pier
National Archives: MT10/1232 Blackpool Central Pier
National Archives: MT10/2012 Blackpool Central Pier
Blackpool Gazette
Blackpool Times
Seven Golden Miles: The Fantastic Story of Blackpool, Kathleen Eyre (author, 1961)
Bygone Blackpool, Kathleen Eyre (Hendon Publishing, 1971)
Uncle Tom's Cabin, Norman Cunliffe (Fylde Historical Society, 1982)
Blackpool Tower, Bill Curtis (Terence Dalton Limited, 1988)
A Tale of Three Piers: A Peep into the past of the Blackpool Piers, Jon de Jonge (Lancashire County Books, 1993)
The Blackpool Story, Brian Turner and Steve Palmer (third edition, Blackpool Corporation, 1994)
Building a Tower, Ron Taylor and Peter Parr (Slate One, 1994)
Blackpool: A Pictorial History, Ted Lightbown (Phillimore, 1994)
Blackpool Pleasure Beach: A Hundred Years of Fun, Peter Bennett (Blackpool Pleasure Beach, 1996)
Blackpool 1897 and the Foudroyant, Cyril Critchlow (author, 1997)
Blackpool, John K Walton (Edinburgh University Press, 1998)
Blackpool Centuries of Progress, Steve Palmer (author, 1999)
The North Pier Story Blackpool, Cyril Critchlow (author, 2002)
Blackpool's Golden Mile, Cyril Critchlow (author, 2006)

Fleetwood Pier
National Archives: BT31/8296/60257
National Archives: MT81/245
National Archives: RAIL1068/92
Fleetwood: A Town is Born, Bill Curtis (Terence Dalton Limited, 1986)
The Fleetwood Story: The Old Town, Bill Curtis and Martin Ramsbottom (Winckley Publishing, 1993)
The Golden Dream, Bill Curtis (CF Publications, n/d)
Fleetwood in old photographs, Catherine Rothwell (Alan Sutton, 1994)
Images of Fleetwood, Bill Curtis (Breedon Books, 1996)

Morecambe Central and West End Piers and Stone Jetty
National Archives: BT31/1373/3787 Morecambe Central Pier
National Archives: BT31/7246/51243 Morecambe Central Pier
National Archives: BT31/31784/37586 Morecambe West End Pier
National Archives: MT10/259 Morecambe West End Pier
The History of Morecambe and Heysham, RC Quick (author, 1962)

The Growth of Morecambe by TF Potter (Morecambe Visitor, 1976)
Magnificent Morecambe, Terry Potter (Carnegie Press, 1989)
Lost Resort? The Flow and Ebb of Morecambe, Roger K Bingham (Cicerone, 1990)
JR Spalding's historical notes on Morecambe (unpublished)

Arnside Pier
Arnside: A Guide and Community History, Dennis Bradbury (author, 2002)

Grange-over-Sands Bayley Lane and Clare House Piers
Grange-over-Sands: The Story of a Gentle Township, WE Swale (author, 1969)
Lancashire North of the Sands, John Garbutt and John Marsh (Alan Sutton, 1991)
Grange-over-Sands Photographic Memories, Robert Swain (Frith, 2005)

Silloth Pier
http://www.solwaybuzz.co.uk

Douglas Iron Pier
http://www.isle-of-man.com
Douglas Centenary 1896–1996, Gordon Kniveton, Robert E Forster, Robert Kelly, Stuart Slack and Frank Cavin (Manx Experience, 1996)

Ramsey Queens Pier
http://www.ramseypier.iofm.net
http://www.theheritagetrail.co.uk
http://www.iomtoday.co.im

Piers That Never Were
Ainsdale – National Archives BT31/9205/68267
Ainsdale – *New Ainsdale – The Struggle of a Seaside Suburb 1850–2000,* Harry Foster (Birkdale and Ainsdale Historical Research Society)
Morecambe Alexandra – National Archives BT31/5461/37774
Southport Alexandra – National Archives BT31/1308/3353

Index